The Diaries
of
John Hunton

MADE TO LAST
WRITTEN TO LAST

Sagas of the Western Frontier

Edited by
Michael Griske

HERITAGE BOOKS
2019

HERITAGE BOOKS

AN IMPRINT OF HERITAGE BOOKS, INC.

Books, CDs, and more—Worldwide

For our listing of thousands of titles see our website
at
www.HeritageBooks.com

Published 2019 by
HERITAGE BOOKS, INC.
Publishing Division
5810 Ruatan Street
Berwyn Heights, Md. 20740

International Standard Book Number
Paperbound: 978-0-7884-3804-2

JOHN HUNTON
&
L. G. (PAT) FLANNERY

JOHN HUNTON
1839 - 1928

Wyoming Pioneer Whose Diaries
Span More Than Half a Century

L . G . (PAT) FLANNERY
1894 - 1964

John Hunton's Neighbor and Close Friend
to Whom He Bequeathed His Diaries

This work is being published to help preserve a factual record of western America's frontier history, and of the men and women who lived in that era.

In Memory of

Billie Griske

Pat Flannery's Daughter
Whose Life Was Once
Saved by John Hunton

SUMMARY OF CONTENTS

Page

Page

ILLUSTRATIONS

PROLOGUE

GOOD FRIENDS, REMARKABLE MEN

I suspect that many frontier history enthusiasts have heard of John Hunton, who was a Wyoming pioneer and prominent businessman in the Fort Laramie area when the post was headquarters for military operations against the Sioux and other Indian nations, as well as being a major crossroads of the Old West. Some might also remember L. G. (Pat) Flannery, my grandfather and Mr. Hunton's good friend despite a 55-year difference in their ages, who was a Wyoming historian, newspaper publisher, statesman, cattle rancher, and veteran of both world wars. A colorful character in his own right, Pat dedicated the last years of his life to historical research and to a special labor of love --- the publication of the diaries kept by Mr. Hunton in which the entries span more than half a century.

My grandfather published the diary entries between 1873 and 1882 in four volumes of 1500 copies each, and two more volumes with entries between 1883 and 1888 were published after his death in 1964. In addition to these daily diary entries, Pat also included narratives by Mr. Hunton and others in these books, and his own painstakingly researched commentaries, to clarify and expand upon events of that period. As a result, the publications vividly preserved day-to-day life on the frontier and presented profiles as well as true exploits not only of people living in that era who have been all but forgotten, but also of such well-known Western folk characters as Wild Bill Hickok, Calamity Jane Canary, Buffalo Bill Cody, Generals Custer and Crook, Red Cloud, Spotted Tail, and many others (most of whom were personally known by Mr. Hunton).

As previously mentioned, Pat initially had only a relatively small number of these books printed. His plan, as I recall, was to pursue republication in larger numbers after the first printings, but he died before having a chance to make this dream a reality. His only child was my mother, Billie Griske, who renewed the copyrights for Pat's works in the 1980's and, in response to numerous requests for the original volumes, republished a few excerpts in small booklets.

After Billie's passing, I decided that I'd also like to share this fascinating and historical material with others. To that end, this book is offered as an abridged and reformatted version of my grandfather's monumental works, with the objective of presenting those excerpts from the original publications that will best paint a vibrant and accurate picture of John Hunton's life, loves, and times as well as appeal to as wide an audience of readers as possible. If John and Pat are judging my efforts from their heavenly perches, I can only hope they're happy with the results.

- Michael Griske -

* * * * * * * * * * * * * * * *

Editor's Notes to the Reader

In the following chapters, John Hunton's diary entries are indented and italicized, and narratives other than those authored by Pat Flannery are in quotes and indented, so that they can be differentiated at a glance from my grandfather's writings. My editorial comments and insertions are bracketed for the same reason.

A brief summary of Pat's life, written by his wife, Alice, for inclusion in volume 5 of the original works, is presented at the end of this book. Unless otherwise indicated, the illustrations for this publication have been provided courtesy of the University of Wyoming's American Heritage Center in Laramie.

John Hunton was often referred to as "Wyoming's Pioneer of Pioneers" by my grandfather, and as "Mr. Fort Laramie" by others, for reasons that should become obvious while reading the following chronicle. I hope you'll enjoy these enthralling sagas of Mr. Hunton's life, old Fort Laramie, and America's western frontier.

CHAPTER 1

A HARD LIFE, BUT SELDOM DULL

John Hunton was born at Madison C. H. (the C. H. being for court house or county seat), Virginia on January 18, 1839 of Alexander B. and Mary Elizabeth (Carpenter) Hunton. Little is known of his childhood. He joined the army at age 18 and saw his first military service at Harper's Ferry in 1859.

Madison was in that borderland between the North and South where the cleavage of loyalties split families, set brother against brother and father against son. Hunton chose the South. He was with Pickett at the charge of Gettysburg and served with the Confederate Army of Northern Virginia until Lee surrendered at Appomattox.

With his homeland overrun and devastated, John Hunton turned his eyes Westward and in the spring of 1867 traveled, via St. Louis and Glassgow, to Nebraska City. From there he whacked bulls on to Fort Laramie, bastion of the plains and headquarters of military operations against the Indian tribes. There he worked for several years as a clerk in the Sutler's store at the old fort, which was to be "home" for the young Virginian for most of the rest of his life.

That first winter, 1867, he shared a room with the famous scout, Jim Bridger, who had been employed by the government to guide our troops. They occupied the northeast corner room of the Sutler's building which was being used as a small hay mow when Mr. Hunton pointed it out to the writer about 1919. At that time the north end of this historic building, made of adobe bricks and understood to be the first permanent structure in what is now the state of Wyoming, was a horse barn. It has since been restored and preserved by the National Park Service. But in 1919 the main room of the old store still had its counters along the walls, there were still some articles of ancient merchandise on its dusty shelves, bundles of undelivered letters in its abandoned post office and a stack of buffalo hides, rotted with age until they tore apart like tissue paper, were piled in one corner of the room from floor to ceiling.

In 1870 Hunton took a contract to supply Fort Laramie with firewood, and his government contracts expanded steadily during the next ten years into big business for that period. In addition to wood he supplied hay, beef, charcoal, lime and other commodities to Fort Fetterman and Camp McKinney as well as to Fort Laramie, and hauled freight with oxen from Medicine Bow Station to Fetterman, Ft. Steele, Ft. Phil Kearney, Ft. Reno, Ft. Smith and other early military installations.

In 1871 he became half owner, in partnership with W. G. Bullock, of the SO cattle, understood to be the first herd in this area, aside from work oxen. This herd, according to Hunton, was started in 1868 by a man named Mills who brought the stock from northern Kansas. [Additional details about Mr. Hunton's "boom to bust" cattle business are presented later in this chapter.]

Hunton was the last post trader at old Fort Laramie; he was one of the first and also one of the last commissioners of Laramie county when it embraced the present counties of Goshen and Platte. Most of the early settlers in that area proved up on their homesteads before him when he was United States Commissioner from 1892 to 1907. As a civil engineer, largely self-taught, he participated in the original survey of north central and western Wyoming when it was mostly an uncharted wilderness area, and he planned and surveyed many of the earliest private reservoirs and irrigation systems in southeastern Wyoming. [John Hunton passed away in 1928.]

Diaries Made and Written to Last

[Although he recorded a few entries in his diary during 1873], it was not until January 1, 1875 that Hunton began to tell in his own words the day-to-day story of his life and experiences. It is a many-sided story: of the cattle industry since its inception in Wyoming; the last of the Indian wars; the passing of the stage coach and the building of the railroads; the disaster of the 80's which spelled finis for the early cattle barons; range wars and homesteading; the gradual development of irrigation, farming, and modern ranching; of history, politics and government.

It is also a tale of life's never-ceasing frustrations for one who seeks perfection; of how a strong man's hopes and ambitions were gradually dimmed and dulled to death by the inexorable years. A story of life as it frequently is, uncolored and un-softened.

The books in which Mr. Hunton kept his early journals deserve a few words. From 1875 until 1900, they are almost identical in form and quality, the only differences being slight variations in color and changes in the printed information they contain. A physical description of the 1875 diary (actually printed for the year 1874) should suffice for all.

This book is 3 x 6 inches in size and solidly bound with a double leather cover. The outside cover has weathered to a deep brown; the inside one retains its natural light-tan freshness and has two leather pockets, front and back. When the double flap of the outside cover is tucked into its slot, the entire book is well-protected against weather and rough treatment when carried in a man's pocket or saddlebag, as this one certainly was on many a rugged journey.

The pages are gold-edged, unfaded, crisp and full of "life" and made of paper built to withstand the effects of water. Hunton

made his entries with both ink and pencil, depending apparently
on whether he was at home or camped on the trail. And not a
leaf in the book is loose from the binding. We do not believe
many present-day papers or bindings possess the same lasting
qualities. [The diaries are now permanently housed at the
University of Wyoming's American Heritage Center in Laramie
as part of the Hunton and Flannery collections donated by the
editor.]

When he made it known that he was leaving his diaries to the
writer, it was requested that the late Dr. Grace Raymond Hebard,
Wyoming historian and head of the State University's department of history, be named joint custodian. After Mr. Hunton's
death, Dr. Hebard and the writer examined the books [which
total more than fifty volumes] and agreed they should be laid
aside for a quarter century. They were kept by Dr. Hebard until
her death and then delivered to the writer, who placed them in a
bank vault until the 25-year waiting period was up.

During his later years, John Hunton became increasingly
reluctant to talk for publication with reporters and writers who
visited old Fort Laramie to interview him. He rather bitterly
resented people weaving bits and pieces of what he said into tales
of their own liking, regardless of how skillfully the job was done.
He wanted his words put down exactly as they were written or
spoken. That was his rule, for he was a blunt and factual man. It
is a rule with which we have tried to keep faith . . . nothing has
been changed, smoothed down, or glossed over.

We assume Mr. Hunton could have had but one reason for
deliberately permitting these records to survive him --- a desire
to preserve from oblivion the true story of his life and his day.
With that thought in mind, we have prepared and present this
work.

Bordeaux - John Hunton's Home

[Located about 27 miles southwest of Fort Laramie], Bordeaux was Hunton's home at that time [that is, when he began to record daily entries in his diaries], and this is perhaps an appropriate place to insert the following summary of a history of Bordeaux, as [conveyed to my grandfather] by Hunton.

In the spring of 1867, the commanding officer at Fort Laramie was ordered to construct a road and telegraph line between Fort Laramie and the newly-established Fort D. A. Russell, near Cheyenne, and dispatched a force of citizen employees with teams, wagons, and equipment to do the work. A military escort of fifty or sixty soldiers accompanied the working party to protect it against hostile Indians, and a government guide, Antoine Ladeau, went along to help select the route.

James Bordeaux, a Frenchman who owned a road house and trading post about nine miles east of Fort Laramie on the Platte River, was tipped off by the guide Ladeau on where the new road would intersect on Chugwater Creek with another new road from Ft. Russell to Fetterman. Bordeaux promptly constructed three connected log rooms at that vantage point, in which he opened a store and road ranch, placing a man named Hugh Whiteside in charge of the new venture.

Whiteside was killed behind his counter by an "outlaw" named Franklin during the winter of 1868. Two men known as "Cy" Williams and Swolley next operated the Bordeaux station for a short time and had a half-breed Sioux Indian boy, Baptiste Ladeau, working for them. [One might speculate that this boy was a relative of the guide, Antoine Ladeau, mentioned earlier, but neither Mr. Hunton nor my grandfather confirmed it as fact.]

On a March morning in 1868, Baptiste Ladeau quit his job and started to Fort Laramie on his pony, with his dog following him.

Death also followed him. The boy was overtaken by Williams, Swolley, and another man, according to Hunton, in the neighborhood of Chug Springs, some four miles north of Bordeaux, where they chased him up the side of a rocky bluff and killed him, together with his horse and dog, [for reasons unknown]. The remains were discovered about six weeks later by a detachment of soldiers. The following May, a band of half-breed Indians caught and killed Williams at the Ecoffey & Cuny ranch five miles southeast of Fort Laramie. [More about this revenge killing can be found in chapter 3.] And the man Swolley also disappeared about the same time.

In the fall of 1868, an old bull-whacker, Ed Foucks, got possession of Bordeaux, ran it well, and enjoyed an extensive patronage. Foucks sold to a man named John Barrett in the summer of 1870, and Barrett sold Bordeaux to Hunton on October 28, 1870, who made it his home and headquarters.

Bordeaux continued to be an important stage station, roadside hostelry, and mail distribution center for a wide area until the coming of the railroad in 1887.

Two Women From Worlds Apart

[John Hunton's diaries tell the story not only of his life, but also] of his love for two women who were perhaps as different as any two women can be. The first --- Lallee [shown on the next page], the beautiful French-Indian girl who was Hunton's companion during his early years on the frontier. She was a sister of Baptiste (Little Bat) Garnier, one of General Crook's most trusted scouts, and Hunton's Road Ranch at Bordeaux was "home" for Little Bat from his early boyhood. Although the romance with Lallee was eventually shattered, the close friendship between Hunton and Little Bat remained steadfast to the end of the road. [An account of Little Bat's life is presented in chapter 3.]

The above photograph of Lallee was discovered at Madison, Virginia, Hunton's birthplace, in an old trunk containing various other photographs, papers, and mementos which he had preserved. It was taken, according to printing on the back, by "Kirkland, 292 Ferguson Street, Cheyenne, Wyoming". The larger original photograph shows more clearly the straight, black hair, dark eyes and complexion, the elaborate feathery head dress, ear rings of horse shoe and quirt design, necklace of beads, and the bright patterned costume with its large, beaded buttons. Sometimes the question is asked, why did so many of our pioneers become squaw men? It seems to be a silly question in Mr. Hunton's case, since Lallee was reputed to have been one of the most beautiful women in the territory. We are indebted for this photograph and other courtesies to Miss Mary B. Taylor, who lived with Mr. and Mrs. Hunton for a number of years at old Fort Laramie when she was a young girl, long after it had been abandoned as a military post.

> *Mon, Feb 12 [1877] . . . Had dreams for the last two nights in which women were fighting with knives and pistols in which I was a party.*

This is the second series of violent and strangely prophetic dreams which Hunton felt impelled to record. The first preceded last year's savage war with the Sioux [documented in chapter 2] and the killing of his brother Jim by the Indians [as described later in this chapter], when he --- *"Dreamed of fighting, of being shot at and shooting people, for the last five or six nights"*. Now come these dreams of battle between presumably jealous females in advance of what was possibly the most violent emotional experience in Hunton's life, the breakup of his romance and companionship with Lallee.

> *Fri, Feb 23 [1877] --- Staid at Fort Laramie last night. Got to Ranch before night. Everything all right except Lallee wanted to leave . . .*
> *Sat, Feb 24 --- Lallee insisted on leaving me with all her things. Told her she could go and let her have wagons to take her things to Laramie River. Parted from her without quarreling. Am much hurt at her conduct towards me but think it best that she leave as she is dissatisfied . . .*

Sun, Feb 25 --- Lallee left Ranch but did not take her things with her . . .

Mon, Feb 26 --- Saw Lallee at Post [Ft. Laramie]. Had talk with her about leaving me. She is now rather disposed not to go but I advised her to leave as she has manifested such a dissatisfied disposition.

Tues, Feb 27 --- Am much in distress about Lallee.

Sun, Mar 4 --- Loaded all Lallee's things on wagon and sent her and them to Patton's by Sam Groves. Learned that she has been toying with Joe Morris . . .

Mon, Mar 5 --- Went to Patton's early this morning for the purpose of diverting Lallee from Morris, and get her to stay at Patton's or come to Ranch until I can communicate with Bat (Little Bat Garnier, her brother) and get her to the [Red Cloud Indian] Agency. All her things had been moved to Morris'.

Tues, Mar 6 --- Persuaded Lallee to have her things moved back to Ranch by Patton and she go to Agency first chance. Arranged for her to leave her things at Patton's and go to Agency at once with Pete Richard and party. Tom Hunton [one of John's brothers] to go along. Went to Ranch.

Wed, Mar 7 --- Tom Hunton and Lallee start to Agency . . . I give Tom positive instructions not to bring her back but leave her at Agency or on Laramie when he

> *returned, and to tell Bat all about her*
> *conduct . . .*
> *Mon, Mar 12 --- Louis Richard and*
> *"Bat" arrived from Agency. They met Tom*
> *and Lallee on Running Water. Told Bat*
> *about Lallee's conduct. Joe Morris not to*
> *blame according to all reports I can hear.*

Apparently Lallee's alleged "toying" with Joe Morris (March 4 entry), which is given some substance by the fact that she had her things moved to the Morris ranch when she left Hunton's (March 5), had little if any effect on friendly relations between the two men. Hunton absolves Morris from fault in the matter (March 12) and [on March 16] loans him his bay colt to ride on a roundup.

[Although Lallee seems to have precipitated the breakup with Hunton], these were the days when white men were beginning to discard their squaws and pack them off to the reservation, frequently keeping the children. There are still a few old timers left who can tell grim tales of babies being literally torn from the breasts of their mothers, who were carried away screaming. Some of them lost their minds, others their considerable pride and thereafter consorted with whomsoever would have them. It is said that these no-longer-wanted Indian women had been, for the most part, faithful and loyal helpmates to their white men, and that their mother love was fierce and strong.

> *Wed, June 13 --- 'L.' went to Laramie*
> *River . . .*

Assuming that "L." was Lallee, it would appear that this young French-Indian woman, now footloose and fancy free, made it clear in short order that she had no intention of settling down

- 15 -

with the Indians on their reservation, as Mr. Hunton obviously
intended she should.

> *Mon, June 25 --- On arriving home*
> *found that Lallee had left with all her*
> *clothes and beding . . .*
> *Wed, Jan 30 [1878] --- Staid at Baptiste's*
> *last night. Lallee and Mary with me . . .*

That long ago evening, more than eight months after their
breakup, which Lallee spent with John Hunton at the home of
her brother (Little Bat), is not the only reason to believe that the
bond between those two was not easily or quickly broken.

On October 22, 1955, Mrs. Pauline E. (Smith) Peyton, a
venerable pioneer woman of Douglas, Wyoming, graciously
wrote down some of her childhood memories for us. Among
them were the following.

"Outstanding in my memory (is) an incident that
took place [probably in 1882 or 1883] the last time I
saw Lallee . . . Mr. Hunton and my father, Edwin C.
Smith, had been standing by a wagon talking for
some time when Lallee, whom I admired very much,
explained to my mother that she wore the soft, high
top shoes that were trimmed in red to please
Hunton, who got those shoes for her.

"Childlike, I followed Lallee to the yard and saw
her hold out both hands toward Hunton as she said,
'Lallee go Hunton'. It seemed to me that Hunton's
face had been very dark all the time that morning.
He caught both of her hands in his own and held
them beneath his chin for a few moments, then
threw her hands away saying shortly, 'No, Lallee

can't go'. She went into our house and sat in the same chair all day, refusing to go to our table to eat."

It appears from entries [in 1878] that Lallee has been staying at least part of the time with Hunton at Bordeaux since they broke up and separated last year. Whether Lallee's position there is now that of a cook and domestic servant or whether their closer relationship of former years has been resumed, it is of course impossible to say and would be imprudent to guess. But knowing Mr. Hunton's stern and uncompromising attitude in matters where he considered a principle to be involved, we doubt if things between them could have been as they were before.

Sat, Dec 20 [1879] --- Lallee left . . . Give
L. span horses, wagon, & harness.

Somehow, the above entry seems to have an air of finality about it. John Hunton would not lightly "give" a team of horses, harness, and wagon to anyone. But he did to Lallee, and she left Bordeaux with three companions who presumably were also of Indian blood.

Lallee had a career as a ranch cook for many years and "took up" with a number of other men after she and Hunton parted. Dim rumor has it that her romances were not long lived. [However, Mrs. Omie Smith, daughter of the late pioneer John R. Smith, wrote that Lallee "worked for our family during the years 1883-4. She was afterward married to Frank Grouard (or Gruard), the government scout stationed at Fort McKinney" and identified by my grandfather as a half-breed Hawaiian who passed for a Sioux.] Lallee grew into a still handsome but large and remarkably powerful woman. It is said that she could, with no apparent effort, snatch a hundred pound sack of flour from a wagon and carry it into her kitchen with one hand.

Following are excerpts from Mr. [Harold J.] Cook's letter of March 16, 1955 [to my grandfather about Lallee in later years].

"... My father, James H. Cook ... knew John Hunton, Lallee, and most of the men mentioned in his most interesting diary.

"Lallee worked for us ... on our ranch here when I was a boy, in the early 90's ... I knew her very well and have jotted down many reminiscences about her during that period ... As I remember her, she was still a very fine, striking looking woman ... very large and robust ... and a *powerful* woman.

"I have seen her do many things that took more muscle than most men have, and do them easily. Her white and Indian blood seemed to crop out at different times in different ways, in what she liked to do and how she did them. She still had some of the things she had when she lived with Hunton, when she was here. Of course, father and mother knew her then and, within limits, she would often talk of those days with them when the mood happened to hit her.

"While she could and would at times dress up as white women do, she generally preferred to wear moccasins that she made herself. She was an expert at leather work and tanning and in doing exceptional "beady work" as she called it, which she taught my mother to do. We have some of her bead work here now.

"I am particularly sorry that my father could not have seen this [referring to the photograph shown earlier in this section] before he passed away, as I know what a great kick he would have gotten from it; and it would certainly have stirred up many old memories in him, now lost."

John Hunton never forgot Lallee. A portrait painting of her hung from the wall of his favorite room when he died in 1928.

* * * * * * * * * * * * * *

Sun, Dec 12 [1880] --- Preparing to go East . . .

Mr. Hunton did not know it, of course, but that trip east [to his birthplace of Madison, Virginia] on which he was about to embark proved to be a fateful journey, altering the entire course of his future life, [for it was during this visit that he met] a beautiful southern girl, less than half his years, with whose youth and charm the middle-aged Hunton fell in love at first sight.

Sun, Jan 3 [1881] --- Met a lady on the street [in Madison] in company with Miss Hanigen which made a great impression on me. Think it must be Miss Taylor . . .

Thurs, Jan 13 --- Was introduced to Miss Blanche Taylor the lady I met on the street, whom I think is my Destiny . . .

Thurs, Feb 10 --- Saw Miss Blanche home. My heart was in my mouth all the way and I could not talk.

Sat, Feb 12 --- Attended Miss Taylor's birthday party in the evening . . . A very pleasant time. Believe I am getting a little spoony on Miss T.

Fri, Feb 18 --- Assisted at a 'snide show' given by some young ladies of the place . . . Miss T. took a leading part and looked magnificent as Goddess of Liberty.

Sat, Feb 19 --- Indicated to Miss Taylor would like to take her West and was led to infer she would go.

Sun, Feb 20 --- Went home [from church service] with Miss Taylor. Am positively dead in love with her, which is the first time in my life I really want to marry.

Tues, Feb 22 --- Proposed to Miss Taylor. Accepted. Very happy . . .

Thurs, Mar 10 --- Called on Miss Blanche and was made very happy by obtaining her permission to speak to her father in regard to our marriage, and fixed the time for April 21 . . .

Fri, Mar 11 --- Wrote to Dr. Taylor asking permission to marry his daughter . . .

Sat, Mar 12 --- No reply from Dr. Taylor. Note from Miss B. saying her father objects and that she would tell me all when we met.

Sun, Mar 13 --- Went to church in evening with Miss B. and had a sad talk. Dr. T. objects and we have to postpone our marriage indefinitely, and I believe for all time.

Mon, Mar 14 --- Called on Miss Blanche and had a long farewell talk. She promises to wait and marry me in October. I believe

she will marry Smoot or any other accept-
able man before that time.

[And so the broken-hearted John Hunton returned home to Bordeaux without his beloved Blanche. However, his diary entries indicate that many letters were exchanged between the two after his arrival. Apparently encouraged by the content of her correspondence, he again traveled east.]

Mon, May 9 [1881] --- My trunk was left behind [at Bordeaux] which will delay me a day in going to Washington [D. C.] expressly to meet Blanche.

Thurs, May 12 --- Will try to bring B. back with me but doubt the prudence of the movement. Will be greatly disappointed if she is not there . . .

Tues, May 17 --- Note from B. who arrived [in Washington] this evening. Called to see her. She is somewhat downcast. Talks all love, but acts a little reserved or careless . . .

Wed, May 18 --- Went to Baltimore with B. and her party. Had a very pleasant trip, but B. acts as if something were on her mind that she can't shake off. She's very loving, very reticent, acts as if she wanted me with her and did not want me . . .

Thurs, May 19 --- Did not see B. until eve and then spent a nice evening driving about the city [Baltimore]. She is reserved as if something hangs heavy on her mind. Think it doubtful if we ever marry . . .

Sat, May 21 --- Bid Blanche a sorrowful
goodby this morning . . . Started west . . .

It now appears that both John Hunton and Blanche Taylor are instinctively becoming aware of, and concerned by, their differences in age, temperament and interests which hold them apart. But theirs is not the only case in which such warnings have been ignored by persons in love.

[Another letter-writing campaign followed during the next few months, which, based on the following entries, appears to have led Miss Taylor and her father to lay aside any reservations they had about John Hunton's intentions. Hunton therefore again headed east to Madison.]

Tues, Sept 20 [1881] --- Left Bordeaux
this morning . . . going to Va.

Sat, Oct 1 --- Arrived here [in Madison]
at noon. Visited Miss Blanche. Was kindly
received by Dr. Taylor and family and was
made very happy by learning they were all
willing for me to have my darling B . . .

Wed, Oct 5 --- Was married at 9:30
A.M.

Mon, Oct 17 --- Had photo taken . . .

The above photograph is undoubtedly the one for which John Hunton and his new bride sat on that October day in 1881. It was taken by "Bogardus, 18th St. & Broadway, N. Y."

[And so Mr. Hunton finally brought his "Destiny" home to Bordeaux.] It is probable that young Blanche did not find her new life all she had anticipated. The transition from that more sheltered and feminine-ridden society in which she was raised into the man's world of a still raw frontier must have been rough and have brought upsetting disillusionment to her. And there is no evidence that she fell passionately in love with an expensive new home at Bordeaux which Hunton labored so long to build and furnish for his bride. But they stuck it through together until the end of the road, which is another and a longer story [beyond the scope of this book. Suffice it to say that love and persistence appear to have conquered all.] The writer will never forget Blanche's touching devotion and her constant care of John Hunton in his last almost blind and helpless years.

Brushes With Death

On rare occasions, while jogging along some dusty road behind Mr. Hunton's sturdy driving team, Dutch and Brownie, the old gentleman's customary reserve would break down and he would start to talk, almost as if to himself, of the old days and, sometimes, of his travels with Lallee across the plains and through the mountains he loved so well. At such times, I soon learned that my cue was to keep as quiet as possible. Often the interruption of a single word or question would remove that far-away look and drop the curtain between past and present.

Of Lallee he always spoke with the utmost respect, as indeed he invariably did of all women. He would speak of her closeness to nature, of how sounds in the wilderness, the cry of a bird, the howl of a coyote had for her a special meaning and frequently spoke to her of things that were hidden from him. Of how she could prepare a palatable meal, where a white man alone would have starved, from what nature had placed at hand on the prairie or in the woods, even to digging certain roots, and pounding them into a sort of flour to make a kind of bread.

He told of one such trip, without specifying when or where, but it must have been before he started his journal, during which he almost lost his scalp and well might have had it not been for Lallee's sixth sense, or whatever it was she had that he did not have. When they had been on this journey for some days, she told him several young warriors were on their trail and intended to kill him. He found this hard to believe because there had been no sign of Indian hostility or indication of "war" when they had left Fort Laramie. Nevertheless, he kept a sharp eye thereafter and they headed for home.

That night he recalled they had camped on a hillside next to a ravine and when he got up the next morning, he saw a bear on the far side of the ravine, far beyond accurate gun range of that day. But because he "felt good", he raised his gun and fired just for the sport of it and was astonished to see the bear fall over dead. They continued their way without further incident only to learn on arriving home that there <u>had</u> been a short Indian outbreak and some savage fighting during their absence.

When peace was reestablished, some of the Indians involved gathered at or near Fort Laramie for a feast, during the course of which certain braves arose and told of their exploits during the "war", as seems to have been the custom. One young warrior got to his feet, pointed at Hunton who was present, and told how he and several companions had trailed the white man and his squaw, intending to scalp him. But early one morning as they were approaching his camp, planning their attack, they saw him get up with the sun, shoot far across the valley, and kill a bear. That changed their minds. They decided not to fight the man with such a mighty gun.

Sat, Feb 23 [1878] --- Started to Box
Elder with [George] Powell. Team ran off;
fell out of wagon and broke my left leg . . .

One late winter in the early 1920's, a "ground blizzard" struck the Fort Laramie area. A brittle sun shone overhead, but the wind's biting cold dug deep and visibility on the ground was close to zero. John Hunton, then in his 80's, and the writer were jogging home to the Old Fort from the "Station", which was Hunton's name for the little town of Fort Laramie on the Burlington railroad, about two and one half miles northeast of the abandoned post.

It was one of those days when the blowing snow piles itself into great drifts and covers tracks almost as fast as they are made. We were driving a young, new-broke team to a spring wagon, hauling a little jag of coal. After crossing the old military bridge across the Platte, about all that one could see was an expanse of swirling white. A lonely fence post now and then were the only guides. Part of the time we would be on the old wagon road, part of the time bouncing across the prairie over hidden hillocks and swales while the young team pranced and pressed hard against the bit, eager to be off and get back to that warm stable at top speed.

Mr. Hunton, hanging on to the hand grip of the seat, jolting up, down, and sideways with the wagon, seemed to be enjoying it more than we were --- as though it reminded him of something. The old gentleman turned and peered at us through the opening in the upturned collar of his cowhide coat with a quizzical smile. Perhaps he was curious to see if we were concerned, as indeed we were. And that concern was not noticeably lessened when he shouted into our ear above the whistling storm. "Almost got my everlasting on a day like this!" "How come?" we shouted back.

After the horses were unharnessed and fed and we were warming up by a hot stove, he told us. It went something like this. He said he was driving from Fort Fetterman to his ranch on the Box Elder when the wheels of his wagon struck something and almost overturned. The horses lunged and started to run. In trying to hold them, he lost balance, fell to the ground, and found he could not get up. His leg was broken.

While his traveling companion (who must have been George Powell from the above entry) made his way on foot for help, Hunton lay there from early afternoon until late at night before a rescue party finally found him. He recalled that snow blew over him and figured that may have saved him from freezing to death. He considered that accident about the "closest call" he ever had.

[Although the following narrative from my grandfather's works has nothing to do with these two episodes in John Hunton's life, I thought you might enjoy reading about this "frontier practical joke", so to speak, related to the military bridge mentioned above.]

Strangely enough, Mr. Hunton does not seem to comment on the actual building of this bridge in his diary, but he did tell the writer that during its construction, a feud developed between the engineer in charge of the work and the commanding officer at Fort Laramie, for some forgotten reason. On completion of the structure, this ill feeling, according to Hunton, inspired the C. O. to have his soldiers pile large freight wagons full of rock, haul them onto the bridge, remove the tongues so they could be butted wheel to wheel across its entire length, and let them stand there for several days. When one of the piers settled slightly under the tremendous weight, Mr. Hunton recalled that the hapless engineer had to rebuild it before the commanding officer would accept the job.

A Brother Lost, and Another Close Call

Fri, May 5 [1876] --- Got back to Milk Ranch about sunset. Heard of horses being stolen on Chug & Jim [Hunton] missing. Went to Post [Fetterman] . . .

*Sat, May 6 --- Staid at Post last night. 8
A.M. got telegram announcing that Jim had
been killed by Indians. Started to Chug
[Bordeaux]...*

*Sun, May 7 --- Got to Ranch 2 P.M.
Started to Cheyenne with Jim's remains at
5 o'clock P.M. ...*

*Mon, May 8 --- Staid at Kellys last
night. Got to Cheyenne at 5 P.M. Arrange-
ments [for Jim's funeral] made by Mr.
Fogelsong and Frank Hunter...*

*Tues, May 9 --- In town [Cheyenne] all
day. BURIED JIM.*

The several stories of how Jim Hunton was killed vary considerably in detail. Here is the dispatch sent from Fort Laramie and
published in the *Cheyenne Leader.*

"THE MURDER OF JAMES HUNTON"

" 'Alter Ego', writing from Fort Laramie under
date of May 6, says: The garrison was startled last
evening by news that Indians had, the evening
before, visited [John] Hunton's ranch . . . 26 miles
south of this post, and stolen 30 head of horses.
Besides this, James Hunton, a well-known frontiersman [pictured on the next page] was supposed to
have been killed from the fact that his horse came
galloping to the ranch without a rider. Twenty men
under Lieut. Allison were immediately started in
pursuit of the marauders and it soon transpired that
the report was only too well-founded.

"Mr. Hunton had ridden out into the hills in search of stray stock and some five or six miles from the ranch was evidently surprised by about 30 Indians. From appearance of ground in vicinity it is believed that his horse, in making some terrible bounds to escape, unfortunately stumbled and threw his rider; that Mr. Hunton regained his feet and ran some 50 yards when, catching his foot in a vine, he also stumbled. There he was surrounded and the savages amused themselves by firing eight bullets into his head and body . . . The ground in the vicinity was literally covered with moccasin tracks.

"The savages then endeavored to catch the horse, which is well known all over the frontier as a very superior animal. They ran him until arriving in sight of the ranch, and remained lying concealed until night when they broke into the corral and stole the 30 horses already referred to. Their trail leads in the direction of the Red Cloud Agency, and owing to a "cut off" made by Lieut. Allison, it is not unlikely that he will either strike them before they reach that hive of rascally thieves or else make the pursuit so hot they will be glad to relinquish their boot and scatter to the four winds . . ."

But none of the Hunton horses were ever recovered. Many years later, John Hunton's own account of Jim's killing was written by him for the *Fort Laramie Scout* [my grandfather's newspaper] and published therein on July 28, 1927.

"May 4, 1876, James Hunton, my brother, left my home on the afternoon of that day to go to the ranch of Charles Coffee, on Boxelder creek to get a horse he had traded for. While going down through 'the notch' in Goshen Hole, about half way between the two places, he was waylaid, shot and killed by five Indian boys, who were out on a horse stealing expedition. The Indians then went to my ranch after night and rounded up, stole and drove off every head of horses and mules (38) I owned except my saddle horse, which I had with me. The horse my brother was riding ran and the Indians could not catch him and the next morning was seen on top of the bluff

east of the ranch. Blood on the saddle told the tale
and a searching party found the body that afternoon."

There is reason to believe John Hunton learned some of the
details of his brother's death directly from the very Indians, or at
least one of them, who committed the act. One sultry summer
day in the early 1920's, jogging to the "Station" from Fort
Laramie with Mr. Hunton in his old buckboard, he told the
writer substantially this story.

Some time after his brother's death, when there was again an
uneasy peace between the red men and the white, Hunton was
present at an Indian "feast" --- we do not know the date or place.
He told how on occasions the Indians would gorge themselves
with unbelievable quantities of meat, often to the point where
they would fall over unconscious, as though drunk, and sleep the
clock around where they lay. He also recalled that these same
Indians could travel for days without food and apparently suffer
no serious discomfort or loss of strength.

And at such feasts following the end of hostilities, it was
considered proper and commendable for warriors who had
distinguished themselves to make speeches bragging of their
exploits and telling how they had killed their late enemies. On
this night a young Indian arose and told in gory detail how he
and others had killed Jim Hunton.

John Hunton said simply, "When I heard it, I suddenly saw
red" and he reached for his gun with but one thought, to kill that
Indian. Squatted beside him in that dim circle by the flickering
fire was a young cavalry officer who saw Hunton's move and
grabbed his gun arm by the wrist before he could draw. Without
moving from their places, and apparently unobserved, the two
men struggled silently for a few seconds until Hunton regained
his senses, and sat stoically dead-panned during the remainder of

the evening, as demanded by protocol. The old gentleman observed thoughtfully that had he fired on his brother's killer, the twenty or thirty white men present would undoubtedly have been killed in a matter of seconds by the hundreds of Indians who surrounded them.

So that unknown, quick-witted young officer with a strong grip possibly robbed history of another massacre. We would probably all be surprised if we knew how many momentous events actually hinge on small incidents which seldom find their way into the books.

The Rise and Fall of Fortune

When John Hunton settled down seriously to keeping a daily record of his life and activities, on January 1, 1875, he estimated his assets at $9,000 against debts totaling more than $16,000 and doubted that he would ever get them paid. But the ensuing years saw his emergence as one of the largest government contractors, bull-train freighters and cattlemen on the booming Wyoming frontier.

[As mentioned earlier in this chapter], Hunton took a contract in 1870 to supply Fort Laramie with firewood, and his government contracts expanded steadily during the next ten years to include supplying wood, hay, beef, charcoal, lime and other commodities to Fort Fetterman and Camp McKinney as well as to Fort Laramie, and hauling freight with oxen from Medicine Bow Station to Fetterman, Ft. Steele, Ft. Phil Kearney, Ft. Reno, Ft. Smith and other early military installations. [The influx of soldiers to these posts to wage war against the Sioux and other tribes, as recorded in chapter 2, contributed significantly to John Hunton's financial upswing. For example . . .] July [1876] was quite a month for Hunton. He received a total of $3,695.66 from his business with Uncle Sam.

[Mr. Hunton's military contracts also continued to multiply after the 1876 wars, as evidenced by the following entries in his 1877 diary.]

> *Sat, June 16 --- Heard I was lowest bidder on hay at (Forts) Fetterman & Reno. Accepted Fetterman beef (contract) by telegraph.*
>
> *Fri, June 29 --- Three coach robberies this week aggregating nearly twenty thousand dollars. Received Notice from Chief Q. M. that Fetterman and Reno hay contract has been awarded me.*

[This new hay contract apparently motivated John Hunton to purchase more equipment, as indicated by the following entries which also point out that he took the opportunity afforded by a buying trip to enjoy cultural events and to do some sightseeing.]

> *Thurs, Sept 13 [1877] --- Started to Chicago [from Omaha, the last leg of this journey] to buy hay press.*
>
> *Fri, Sept 14 --- Traveled . . . in company with Gen. Crook . . . Visited McVickers Theatre [in Chicago] and saw Booth in 'Brutus'.*
>
> *Sat, Sept 15 --- Visited Exposition. Saw much machinery and many things new to me. Bought hay press and wire. Visited Hooleys Theatre and saw Barrett in Richard Third.*
>
> *Sun, Sept 16 --- P.M. took carriage and drove about the city. Saw Water Works,*

Lincoln Park, etc. Visited Ellisiumn Thea-
tre . . . Saw the nude beer jerkers.
Mon, Sept 17 --- Visited the Exposition
and other places. Made some purchases.
Went to Hooleys Theatre, saw Barrett in
Julius Caesar.

[Jumping ahead several years . . .] The year 1882 marks the start of a new era in Mr. Hunton's life. His rough-and-ready days as a bullwhacker and frontier squawman are over, and he is embarking on the new year with a brand new bride of half his years. It is a radical change which he seems to find a bit disconcerting at times, but it leads him on to a rapid climb in the business, political and social affairs of the territory.

1883 started off in a somewhat leisurely and luxurious fashion, with Mr. Hunton and his bride, Blanche, on a winter vacation which took in Florida and other southern states [and attested to his rising income]. He returned to Wyoming and buckled down, with energy and apparently considerable planning, to work toward his objective which was to lay the foundation for a land and cattle empire in Wyoming Territory. It was a year in which he entered into numerous partnerships, took the lead in organizing several companies, and started on much new enterprise.

Prior to '83, Hunton had sent his wire fences stretching out from Bordeaux across many miles of public domain --- and this was to become one of the stumbling blocks to attainment of his ambition. There were objections, apparently right from the start, and he spent three days in Washington [D. C.] during January, 1883, conferring with Wyoming's Representative, M. E. Post, and land office officials on the matter of fences.

Throughout the year, he induced a number of friends, relatives and employees to enter homesteads and file desert claims on land embracing stock-water and hay meadows which would give him more or less control over the surrounding range lands and make them next to worthless, without water or winter feed, to other potential users.

On May 1, [1883], his expansion program really got under way when he sold the Teschemachers and DeBillier a half interest in all his holdings on the "Chug" for $55,000. The partnership was known as John Hunton & Co. An interesting feature of this deal is that these partners also agreed to pay $15,000 for a half interest in certain tracts of land Hunton hoped to acquire and add to his holdings, but which were still owned by the United States when the contract was executed.

His next partnership was completed in June when he and F. M. Phillips joined to invest $6,000 or more each in some kind of a deal with the Grants, presumably father and son Robert and Duncan Grant, for their cattle and land.

Two months later, on August 23rd, Hunton and E. W. Whitcomb formed a co-partnership and purchased the Joe Knight cattle herd for $120,000. A man named Farlough (or Farleigh) was apparently part owner of these cattle.

In September, he joined with the London brothers, Hiram B. Kelly, and Colin Hunter in financing an exploratory survey for an irrigation ditch from the Platte River, and employed George A. De Hennecourt (or De Hanicourt) to do the work. This preliminary survey showed the job to be much larger and more expensive than anticipated, so the pioneer group incorporated, forming the N.P.D.&I. Co. (presumably the North Platte Development and Irrigation Co.). In October, this company hired W. C. Bradbury & Co. to do the construction work. Judging from the amount of beef, hay, grain, and other supplies purchased by this firm at Bordeaux during the remainder of the year, Mr. Bradbury must have moved in a substantial crew of men and stock to build this ditch.

On November 9, John Hunton took on another partnership with A. B. Clarke to buy a hundred head of cattle from Mr. Draper, for which they paid $1000 down and gave their notes for the balance of $2500.

This summary does not include a number of personal business deals in which Mr. Hunton purchased cattle, horses and equipment for his rapidly expanding operations. And at the year's end, he appears to have been prosperous, confident, and sure of himself. But there were a few small clouds on the horizon. One of his claims on the Platte Meadows, filed in the name of Paddleford, was being seriously contested, requiring his presence in the "land court" at Cheyenne for several days. And most significant of all, he learns from his newspaper on December 23rd that the federal government has brought suit against him and Hi Kelly to force removal of their fences from the public domain. So he hustles over to Cheyenne the very next day and enters filings on seven more desert land claims, presumably to strengthen his rights and position in the suit.

Why did John Hunton thus expand himself and involve his affairs with so many others in such a short period of time? Who can say? But the cattle barons were rising and it is possible he decided that rapid expansion was necessary to hold his place in the sun. Perhaps it should also be said, in fairness, that in the opinion of this writer at least, Mr. Hunton appears to have been only trying to follow in a small way strictly modern business practices whereby a few estimable and emulative gentlemen of today, through great corporate combinations with interlocking directorates, manage to dominate and control much of the nation's commerce and industry. It remains to be seen, of course, whether what eventually happened to Hunton's dream of empire could also happen to more modern, complex, and involved business structures, should the wheel of fortune chance to take a few bad turns, as it did in his case. [Many corporate "bad turns" have, indeed, been exposed after my grandfather wrote this passage, giving credence to the old adage that the more things change, the more they stay the same.]

During ten months of 1884 (the financial records for July and August are missing), John Hunton recorded receipts of $74,700 and expenditures of more than $79,000. And these figures undoubtedly fail to reflect substantial business transactions of the several partnerships and companies in which he was interested. For a period of some years, Mr. Hunton's records indicate that he spent considerably more cash than he took in. But that was probably more than offset by book value increases in the worth of his cattle and other holdings. So all continued to go well.

[An offspring of the Wyoming cattle boom during these times was the Cheyenne Club --- pictured above.] Among the books preserved by John Hunton is an exquisitely printed, red leather bound, five-by-seven inch volume of forty-two pages. Embossed on the cover in gold letters is, "The Cheyenne Club, 1891". This little book contains the rules, names of officials, members, etc. of that remarkable group from the date of the club's founding in 1880.

This photograph of the most famous and fabulous cattlemen's club in history [courtesy of the Wyoming State Archives and Historical Department] was taken about 1888 when it was young, and preserved by Russell Thorp of Cheyenne. In later years, improvements were added and those young trees in the foreground grew tall, shading its wide verandas.

The Cheyenne Club, perhaps the wealthiest and most exclusive organization on the frontier, stood at the corner of Seventeenth Street and Warren Avenue. Its founders and early membership were, to a considerable extent, young men from prominent and wealthy families in the eastern United States, the British Isles, and Europe. Some of them were world travelers, recent graduates of famous universities --- and perhaps a few were well-heeled "remittance" men, banished to the new West by their families for various reasons. But [Mr. Hunton and the other members] all had certain purposes in common, one being to get rich quick raising cattle on the lush, wide and free ranges of Wyoming Territory.

Although sport, pastime and amusement were the avowed original purposes of this club, there is no denying that within its walls much history was made. Perhaps no other single group played such a controlling and influential part in shaping the early patterns of Wyoming political, economic, and social life. Its membership was also a substantial core of the Wyoming Stock Growers Association, an organization around which much early history revolves, and which remains to this day one of the most powerful political and economic groups in the state.

It was a place of luxurious living. Its members entertained the elite of society, world-famous celebrities of the day, and nobility from many lands --- with rare wines and exotic viands gathered from around the world. It was a place of romance, adventure --- and intrigue. But such tales will not be retold here --- they would make a fascinating book of their own.

In December, 1928, historian John Clay, casting back with nostalgia to the old days, mused on how the Cheyenne Club was born, the gay and carefree life it housed, and how it gradually declined into oblivion after the cattle bubble was punctured, marking the end of an era. True, in 1928 Mr. Clay and a few other old timers still maintained rooms in the ancient clubhouse but, as he wrote: " . . . the glory has departed . . . the brave band dispersed . . . the rooms seem haunted. The harp that played there is silent now, but its echoes still vibrate."

[And now we return to John Hunton . . .]

Fri, Feb 20 [1885] --- Had talk with Sturgis and J. W. Hammond about the land grabbers on Black Thunder.

The "land grabbers" on Black Thunder were probably some of the early smaller settlers who flocked into northeastern Wyoming. They were vicariously called nesters and rustlers as well as settlers and homesteaders, according to which side you were on. The feud between these people and the large cattle interests, who dominated the open range prior to their coming, culminated in the "Johnson County War" of 1892.

Regardless of the merits and morals involved in that bitter episode, these newcomers certainly had no monopoly on "land grabbing" during this period. Just about everybody who could was doing it, or trying it. The biggest land grab of all, of course, was when the white men wrested the country from the Indians in violation of every treaty. Next a comparative handful of big cattlemen, of whom Hunton was one, sought to corner the free and open range for their vast and growing herds.

In his diary entries, Mr. Hunton tells quite frankly of his own efforts in that direction [as previously indicated]. Now come the small home seekers and settlers, each seeking a slice of the pie in this new land. The friction and strife that resulted was inevitable. The men of each competing group undoubtedly thought, according to their own light and viewpoint, that they were right. It was just another chapter in the continuing struggle for advantage and survival which men of all generations seem doomed to wage, in one form or another, among themselves.

[On August 8, 1885], President Grover Cleveland issued a proclamation making it unlawful to fence in public lands, "obstructing free passage and transit". This proclamation marked the beginning of the end for those far-flung cattle outfits which depended on free and exclusive use of vast areas of the open range for their existence. However, they apparently did not recognize it at the time as handwriting on the wall. Mr. Hunton does not even mention the proclamation in his diary.

1885 was a big money year for John Hunton, the only trouble being that he was headed in the wrong direction so far as finances were concerned. He took in $70,000 but apparently spent more than $90,000, leaving him some $20,000 on the short end of the stick. But apparently he was not much worried --- not yet.

Meanwhile, the progress of events was slowly but inexorably moving to end the absolute rule of those early cattle barons over the great western public domain, as indicated by the following article from the Cheyenne *Democratic Leader.*

" PRESIDENT ALARMED
BY 'LAND GRABBING' "

"New York, April 22, 1886. --- There is a rumor
the President has been making one of those careful
and laborious studies to which he is given, of the
public land question, and that he has become so
thoroughly convinced of the vastness of the misuse
of present laws for land-grabbing by syndicates and
corporations . . . that he will presently send a special
message to Congress, urging immediate action in the
way of reform and repeal of bad laws to help him in
saving the still remaining lands for homesteads for
the people."

On January 1, 1887, John Hunton and his young wife were
prominent in Cheyenne's top-flight society. He had climbed the
ladder of success in a new land to become one of the Territory's
influential leading citizens, with the reputation as a man of
character and integrity --- and he had just been elected a
commissioner of Laramie county, which included most of
southeastern Wyoming and Cheyenne, the Territorial Capital
and center of its wealth and population. In fact, Cheyenne had
gained a reputation of being the nation's richest city, per capita,
and some also said the most wicked. But now John Hunton's
diary is leading into dismal days.

A terribly severe winter had engulfed the Wyoming plains
toward the end of 1886. It loosened its grip for a little while in
mid-January, but that January thaw, instead of proving to be a
blessing, turned out to be the winter's gentle accomplice to
killing. It paved the way for a final fatal blow to the great early
herds and their owners. It was the "great chinook" which melted
the winter's deep snows so quickly that meadows and valleys,

where most of the feed lay, were turned into mushy, shallow lakes almost overnight. Then winter closed in again, with more blizzards, intense prolonged cold and bitter winds, locking the grass under an armor of flint-like ice and crusted snow which the starving herds could not penetrate. And so the cattle died by the thousands. And the great syndicates and "barons", already under pressure from declining prices and tightening credit, went down financially even as their suffering livestock gave up the ghost on those cruel, bare ranges.

> *Wed, Feb 9 [1887] --- On street [in Cheyenne] most of the day but done some writing and made estimates of lumber for store at Chug. Employed Architect Mathews to draw plans for hotel, am to pay him $95.*

Despite mounting debt, John Hunton is apparently willing to plunge and gamble still further on Wyoming's future, so now he plans to build a store at Chugwater and a hotel at Bordeaux. He knows that the Cheyenne & Northern railroad will soon reach these points and must have had the assurance that a station would be built at Bordeaux, thus making it a transfer point from the rails to the stage lines bound for Fort Laramie, the Black Hills, and other places.

More stories about the weather and cattle from the *Cheyenne Leader* of March 10th.

" FETTERMAN'S WINDIEST WINTER "

"Charles Rastetter, who arrived in this city from Fort Fetterman yesterday, states that the past winter has been the windiest he has ever seen in this

country, and the worst ever known around Fetterman. He reports that from October 24 to February
20 the wind blew with almost hurricane force every
day and during the time it also snowed."

"DRIFTING CATTLE
ROAM CHEYENNE STREETS"

"There are . . . a number of cattle roaming at large
in Cheyenne, and when interviewed yesterday on
the subject, some of the politicians said there was no
longer any use trying to keep them within bounds.
(The poor things, desperate for shelter and something to eat, were drifting in from the barren,
windswept ranges.) This is perhaps well enough for
this time of year, for there is little damage to be done
by the strolling animals at present . . . It should be
remembered that only by degrees does a town
become entirely metropolitan."

That terrible winter, coupled with a lot of fast and loose
speculation, literally washed away the sand-like financial
foundations of those early cattle barons. But they were able and
determined men not easily discouraged or put down, and amid
the ruins of disaster, some were already dreaming of new and
greater worlds to conquer --- of a vast six-state, monopolistic,
livestock-public domain combine such as this nation has never
known, and such as the world may never know except perhaps in
some realm of communism or other form of unprecedented
monopoly.
Here is how the press reported that dream.

" STOCK GROWERS PLAN
SIX-STATE SYNDICATE "

"June 2, 1887: The St. Louis *Globe Democrat* . . . gives an account of a gigantic scheme to consolidate all the cattle interests of the Northwest and form a company which shall control . . . $10,000,000 worth of cattle and grazing lands . . . It will unite Wyoming, Colorado, eastern Utah, western Nebraska, southern Montana and South Dakota. It seems to have originated with the Wyoming Stock Association in Cheyenne and is the outgrowth of the combination of smaller cattle companies which had been going on for several years.

"The scheme . . . for organizing the largest cattle company ever known would control ranges larger than many states. Periodic depressions, necessitating the weaker ranchmen to sell unmatured stock at ruinous prices, have been disastrous at times. The consolidation (it is believed) will . . . relieve this.

"The fear of the disasterous consequences of recent failures compelled the cattlemen to take immediate action, and delegates were sent to New York, London, and Edinburgh. Those connected with the enterprise are Sturgis, Davis, Clarke [probably one of Hunton's partners] of Cheyenne, Oelrichs and Havemeyer of New York, together with a number of Scottish and British capitalists and some from Boston and Philadelphia. These gentlemen already control fully half the stock in Wyoming."

But their grandiose dream was not to be. They probably did not realize it, but the trend was to be away from "bigness" for a while. The day of the small homesteader and homebuilder was dawning --- and with it was to come much bitter violence on the range. [My grandfather's passing precluded his further discussion of these matters in his manuscripts, so we must leave that to other historians.]

More news stories of the day:

" CHICAGO FEARS BEEF FAMINE "

"A Chicago newspaper estimates that the 'hard winter' of 1887 took 400,000 head of cattle in Montana, 100,000 in Idaho, 300,000 in Wyoming and 50,000 in Colorado. The actual total, if known, might exceed a million head. To make matters worse, 50 to 75 percent fewer calves will be born next spring."

" RUINOUS CATTLE PRICES
ALARM BUSINESS WORLD "

"Great uneasiness, such as has never before prevailed, is manifest in business circles over the low market price of cattle. In Chicago over 200,000 head have been thrust on the market in the last 30 days. The price of thin cattle . . . is outrageously low as the markets are flooded with that class of stock."

Thurs, Sept 22 [1887] --- Come here today [to Cheyenne] on train. Several trains cattle shipped from Uva.

That was not a very good time to ship cattle, but possibly the owners had no choice. A press dispatch tells why: *"Chicago, September 22, 1887: The cattle market has now touched the lowest point yet."* But despite all his worry, discouragement, sleeplessness and hay fever, John Hunton, while staring bankruptcy in the face, has somehow managed to complete his new hotel building on the new railroad at old Bordeaux [shown below in a photo from the Colorado State Historical Society].

[According to Mr. Hunton's journal, it appears that besides the devastating winter of 1886 -'87], his money troubles were due to a mountain of accumulated debt, a tightening of credit and disastrously low cattle prices, coupled with a general business depression. [During the 1880's], he spent thousands of dollars more each year than he took in --- not personally or in riotous living, but on the expansion and development of his land and cattle empire, the building of irrigation works, the financing of "homesteaders" and the purchasing of their claims when they "proved up", etc.

And all went well so long as prices continued to rise or held steady, and he could obtain credit on which to operate. No doubt his books showed substantial paper profits during those boom years. He was already a man of substance, and well on his way to moderate wealth by the standards of his day, when the bubble burst. He can now no longer raise money even for actual living expenses, much less to satisfy a host of demanding creditors, also in dire straits. He cannot go on much longer, and knows it. It is probable that most other Wyoming cattlemen, and businessmen too, found themselves in the same predicament, and for the same reasons during that disastrous year of 1887.

> *Mon, Oct 10 [1887] --- M. E. Post & Co. failed.*

Failure of the banking house of M. E. Post, where Hunton obtained much of his credit in happier and more prosperous years, was perhaps a natural and to-be-expected consequence of the general bankruptcy which prevailed in the cattle industry, upon which most of the loans and business of this bank were undoubtedly based. [An 1892 editorial in the *Cheyenne Leader* reported that former cashier John W. Collins had just been arrested and charged with, among other things, "deliberately and wantonly" ruining the Post Bank. Despite an earlier testament from Morton Post that he "faithfully discharged his trust and that he has merited my best regards", Mr. Collins committed suicide a few days after his arrest.]

1887 ended with the empires of the "cattle barons" crashing on all sides, including that of the Swan clan, perhaps the largest of them all. In December, Hunton was called upon, as county commissioner, by Sheriff Sharpless to help appraise the cattle, land and other property of the Wyoming Hereford Association, another of the great ones. The broke ranchers, credit and resources exhausted, had no choice but to liquidate what they had left for whatever it would bring.

Hunton saw no hope ahead. The depths of his despondency is shown by the following 1888 entries in his diary.

> *Sun, Jan 1 --- Feel that my life has been a failure and that I will never recover financially...*
>
> *Sat, Jan 7 --- Tried to borrow some money [in Cheyenne] but failed...*
>
> *Tues, Feb 7 --- Have many calls for money but cannot pay my bills...*
>
> *Fri, May 4 --- I am mad, damn mad, mad enough to commit any crime [a very uncharacteristic thought for the honorable Mr. Hunton]...*
>
> *Mon, June 18 --- Done some writing and some standing off of creditors.*
>
> *Wed, June 27 --- Discharged [Hunton employees] Hayes & wife at noon --- have not got money to pay them...*

August 4 is the last entry in John Hunton's diary for 1888 --- the rest of its pages are blank. One can only surmise as to why he cut it off sharp, breaking a habit of 15 years. Perhaps that crisis, that "going broke" he had been expecting and predicting for months, suddenly came to a head. It may have just been too painful to write about.

And he left no diary for 1889, either --- the only full year of which there is no record during more than half a century. Again, one can but speculate. Did he fail to keep a diary in 1889, or did

- 48 -

he make the record and then destroy or lose it? It was a year of
financial "come down" for John Hunton --- from the top to near
the bottom of the ladder --- that much we know. It may have
been a year of desperate efforts and deals to stave off ruin, the
record of which he thought it best not to preserve. In the
complete absence of any diary for 1889, the following excerpts
from a letter dated May 5th of that year to Mr. G. H. Taylor of
Madison, Virginia, graphically paints the stark picture of
financial disaster which has overtaken John Hunton (and
practically all of the early cattle "barons") in the wake of that
killing winter of 1886-'87, coupled with their "blue sky" business
practices.

" . . . Quite a change has come over my
circumstances since I last saw you. The change in
dollars amounts to about $210,000. When I was last
in Virginia I was reputed to be worth nearly a
quarter million --- I was offered $190,000. Today I
cannot pay my debts. I am trying to start fresh and
have a place that I am making a little money at but it
comes awful slow.
"I have never told Blanche exactly how hard up I
am and we still manage to live comfortably and
cheerfully. Since I have been appointed Post Trader
[at Fort Laramie] and made my home here I have
given up the management of the [Bordeaux] Ranch
to Mr. [F. O.] deBillier and only go there about every
two months.
"Stock business of every kind is very dull and
getting more so every day. A great many cattle are
being shipped from Texas, New Mexico & Arizona to
northern Wyoming, Dakota, & Montana. This country has been overstocked and eat out. Cattle are very

The Diaries of John Hunton

Made to Last, Written to Last

cheap . . . I sold all the horses I had a few days ago (some 300 head of mares, colts & others) for $35 per head on time, half in 12 months and half in two years . . . "

His former wealth and property were never regained, but John Hunton never lost his reputation as a gentleman of strong character and integrity and as one of the most accurate historians of his time. [He went on to pursue other careers, as touched upon at the beginning of this chapter, and] . . . left behind him monuments of accomplishment in many fields instead of dollars.

Saving Little Billie With a Steady Hand

[Pat Flannery's death in 1964 left unpublished any narratives he might have written about John Hunton's life beyond the times already discussed, at least for the most part. However, the following episodes from Mr. Hunton's twilight years were, in fact, recorded by my grandfather in his manuscripts and give us a glimpse of his protective and loving relationship with Pat's daughter --- my mother Billie.]

On one hot day [in the summer of 1922], we had finished giving our work horses their noon feed in the old Sutler's store building --- part of which had been converted into a stable --- and stepped forth, all unsuspecting, into the bright sunshine and a soul-chilling experience. Although today rattlesnakes are a rarity on the site of old Fort Laramie, surrounded as it is by irrigated fields and meadows, they were not so rare forty years ago, and it paid a man to keep his eyes and ears open.

A hundred feet or more from that stable door, in back of the "Burt House" where we lived, there was a stock watering tank around which our baby daughter loved to play. We noticed her sitting on the ground, leaning forward and chopping at something with her little toy hatchet. Then we froze with horror, as in a nightmare. She was slowly inching herself ahead and chopping away at a rattlesnake, coiled and ready to strike, just a few feet beyond her reach. John Hunton had also seen, from his window next door, and before we could make a move, he stepped around the corner of the building, raised his Webley [a .442 caliber revolver] with hand steady as a rock despite his more than 80 years, and cleanly shot off the snake's head.

It is not surprising, in retrospect, that John Hunton had a watchful eye on our daughter, for something of a love affair had developed between them. Quite often, on nice days, he would present himself at our kitchen door and ask if little Billie could go walking with him. Little Billie was generally eager to and her mother, as a rule, freely gave her consent, knowing her daughter could not be in safer hands.

So it became a familiar sight to see that very old man and that very little girl strolling hand in hand about the old parade ground and in and out among the ghostly lime-concrete ruins of what had once been Officers Row. On their frequent stops to rest they would sit, heads close in earnest talk about whatever it is very old men and very young girls talk about. But we did not realize the part this played in his lonely life until many, many years later --- long after he was gone.

That summer my wife gave a birthday party for our daughter, and little boys and girls came from miles around, bringing their parents with them. There was much turning of ice cream freezers that afternoon. Much woman talk in the house and man talk outside in the shade. The kids splashed in the river, screamed, and cried, played and fought, had fun in their own way.

Just a few years ago, reading Mr. Hunton's diary for this period, we came across an entry which went something like this.

Billie's mother gave a birthday party for her today. Many came. I was not invited but Billie brought me a piece of her birthday cake.

You would have been invited, Mr. Hunton, had we realized. You should have been invited. Without your steady hand on that sturdy old gun, there might not have been a birthday party for the little girl of whom we both were fond.

CHAPTER 2

- *FRONTIER WARFARE* -
A TRAGIC AND FEARSOME THING

[As previously indicated, John Hunton and my grandfather used to "ride the range" together in a buckboard on business or just for relaxation. During these outings, Mr. Hunton would occasionally speak of his life, times, and views, including the following perspective sympathetic to Native Americans that echoes reasons discussed in this chapter's narratives for their adoption of savage ways.]

On one of our rides together, Mr. Hunton expressed himself to the writer as considering the white man primarily responsible for the Indian wars. He said the tribesmen were originally a dignified, trusting people who kept their word and agreements and were inclined, for the most part, to be friendly until after they had been lied to, cheated and treated with contempt by their white brothers, or at least by some of them. But he also pointed out that once their confidence had been destroyed, the Indians not only learned and embraced the civilized arts of treachery and deceit --- they added to them certain distinctive techniques of savage cruelty and cunning which made warfare on the plains a fearsome thing.

A Brief History of Old Fort Laramie

[The following passages were written by John Hunton for the *Goshen News*, another of Pat Flannery's newspapers. Pat later published them in small booklets for Wyoming history buffs.]

FORT LARAMIE (Circa 1876)

Photograph Courtesy of the
National Park Service and the
National Archive and Records Service

"From all information obtainable there cannot, I think, any written history of Fort Laramie be found prior to 1923 or 1924. I think all accounts of the place before that time are embraced in such letters, memoranda and 'word of mouth' as have been gathered by the story writers.

"Legend says: That about 1815 or 1816 a man named La Ramie appeared in the country with a small band of trappers and engaged in trapping on the river and its tributaries and finally located at what is now the Old Fort. That about 1819 or 1820 he went up the river in the fall of the year to trap and was never seen again. It was subsequently learned through the Arapahoe Indians that he was killed by them and his body put under the ice in a beaver dam near the mouth of Sybil Creek. After that time the river was called Laramie's River and the peak Laramie's Mountain. All places and things called Laramie took the name the same way.

"When many more trappers and fur hunters began to appear in the country, one of the principal men was William Sublett. The place was then for some years called Fort William, in honor of Mr. Sublett. In the meantime, another fur trading company had established itself at a point about a quarter of a mile south of the south end of the bridge across the Platte. It was called Fort John. It was quite a fur trading post for some years, but finally quit business. About 1834 the ownership of Fort Laramie (often called Fort William) was merged into the American Fur Company and was owned by different groups of men until about June 1849, when it was purchased from the agent of the American Fur Company, Mr. Bruce Husband, by Lt. Woodberry for the Government of the United States, for the sum of $4,000.00, and has had no other name since that date.

"The front part of the old Sutler's store was constructed in 1849. Bedlam, [the bachelor officers' quarters], was constructed the year following.

"Three companies of cavalry arrived at the Fort on June 22, 1849, and one company of infantry. Company 'G', 6th Infantry --- which was destined to be the permanent garrison for many years --- did not arrive until August 12th, as it had to perform escort duty for a large ox train. The first chaplain and teacher arrived there in 1849 and remained until 1862.

"There were, during very much of the time from the beginning of the Fort up to 1872, a great many Indians in its immediate neighborhood. After the big Indian Agency was established thirty miles down the Platte River from the Fort, in 1871, there were not so many. There was always more or less Indian excitement in the neighborhood from 1855 to 1877. Although it never was seriously threatened, many persons were killed and their property destroyed and stock run off within a few miles of the Fort. The last killing by Indians known to have occurred in what might be called the Fort Laramie neighborhood took place on the Big Bitter Cottonwood Creek, near the Coleman Ranch, in March 1877.

"There were, at one time, a great many Indian children buried on the trees near the mouth of Dean Creek by lashing a few poles on the limbs of the trees, thus making a scaffold on which the corpse was laid and wrapped securely in robes or skins to the scaffold, tied with rawhide and left to its fate. Many of them were buried on scaffolds set on posts about 8 feet above the ground. A few hundred yards north of where the Fort Hospital stood was a favorite place for this mode of burying. Chief Spotted Tail's daughter [Fallen Leaf, whose poignant story is told in chapter 3] was buried there in the spring of 1866.

"[After] . . . many interesting and exciting occurrences took place at Fort Laramie, it was abandoned in 1890. The original order for abandonment was issued in 1889, and headquarters and two companies of the 7th Infantry went to Fort Logan, near Denver, early that fall, being immediately followed by two other companies. The remainder of the garrison stayed until April, 1890. About the 1st of March, 1890, a detachment of about 20 cavalry soldiers and ten or twelve citizen mechanics, under command of Lieutenant C. W. Taylor, Quartermaster of the 9th U. S. Cavalry, arrived at the Fort and at once commenced to dismantle the buildings by taking off doors, windows, hardwood flooring and such other material as was thought to be of value to the Government. After this job had been completed, all the buildings except one set of officers' quarters, which was occupied by Mr. John Field, the custodian, were sold at auction to different citizens [including Hunton] and became private property. The last soldiers left the Fort on Sunday morning, April 20th, 1890.

"The Military Reservation was nine miles long, north and south, and six miles wide. It was surveyed during the summer of 1891 . . . and opened up for entry and settlement on October 5th, 1891, to homesteaders . . . "

[The old Fort Laramie post has now been designated a National Historic Site, with some of its buildings restored under the National Park Service's wing. I often thought I could almost feel the spirits of soldiers and others from John Hunton's time hovering over those historic grounds during my many visits to this site in my youth. Perhaps you can, too, if you decide to make the trip.]

The Grattan Massacre

[My grandfather described the following events in his books even though they took place a few years before John Hunton came to Fort Laramie. However, this narrative sets the stage for Pat's other passages about the quarter-century of hostilities on the plains that the massacre precipitated and their significant impact on Mr. Hunton's life, all of which started with the seemingly trivial killing of a "lame and half-starved old cow" abandoned by its emigrant owner.]

The Laramie River flows into the North Platte about two miles below (east) of Fort Laramie. Starting some distance below this point, their lodges stretching for miles along the Platte, was an encampment of several thousand Indians, various bands and tribes of the Sioux Nation. The year was 1854. It was the month of August.

They had gathered for their annual handout of goods and supplies, due them from the United States government under treaty. The date set for distribution was long past. They had been waiting for weeks. Their goods were stored several miles upstream in a warehouse at what was known as the Gratiot Houses, a trading post also called Fort John, a short distance east of Fort Laramie --- but the Indian Agent, Major J. W. Whitfield, had not arrived to issue them. Each day the Indians had to drive their ponies a greater distance for grass. Each day their hunters had to range in ever-widening circles in search of game for the cooking pots. They were understandably restless and provoked.

Also running near the Platte, almost within sight of these Indians, was the emigrant route generally known as the Oregon Trail, over which an almost constant stream of covered wagons plodded their weary way westward. This trail was known among the Indians as "The Holy Road" because of the terms of a treaty between the Sioux and the white men made on Horse Creek, near Fort Laramie, in 1851. This treaty provided that the red men would not attack or molest the white man's wagon trains traveling this trail; that if Indians should steal from the emigrants, the chiefs would see that full restitution was made; that if the whites stole from the Indians, the government would recompense them for their loss. In return for this safe passage, the United States promised to issue the Sioux tribes $50,000 worth of goods each year --- delivery to be made near Fort Laramie. It was a touchy situation, an uneasy truce, marred by some incidents on both sides --- but it worked pretty well, the wagon trains had gotten safely through, until this lame and half-starved old cow came staggering along on August 18, 1854.

She belonged to a wagon train which left her behind when she could no longer keep up. A young Miniconjou brave named High Forehead, on his way to visit the camp of the Brules nearby, discovered the cow, down, helpless and apparently abandoned. He promptly slaughtered her, summoned some of his Brule friends, and they had a feast. The wagon train proceeded to Fort Laramie, where the owner of the cow reported her stolen by Indians and demanded compensation.

Conquering Bear, chief of the Brules, also heard of the incident and realizing it might be considered a violation of the treaty, immediately went to Fort Laramie and offered a pony as restitution for the cow. Old records indicate that a good horse was worth at least two good cows along the trail.

Unfortunately, most of the officers and men on duty at Fort Laramie were absent, leaving only a skeleton garrison in the post and Lt. Hugh B. Fleming in temporary command. Lt. Fleming, a young officer, was apparently reluctant to make a decision in the matter and Conquering Bear, unable to get an answer to his offer, returned to his camp and held a night conference with other head men. Early next morning, Man Afraid of His Horses ---

although some translations say it should be Man Afraid of His Woman --- a sort of over-chief among the Sioux, returned with a small delegation to the Fort and renewed the offer. Again they could get no decision from Lt. Fleming, who left them cooling their heels all morning and into the early afternoon.

Now comes the most amazing and difficult to understand part of the whole proceedings. Although refusing to accept full restitution for the cow as the treaty provided, Lt. Fleming instead authorized Lt. John L. Grattan to take a detail to arrest High Forehead, which he had not authority to do, and then washed his hands of the whole affair. Grattan, a green and hot-headed 24-year-old, just graduated from West Point, started celebrating his first command with a bottle while assembling his expedition --- a wagon, two 12-lb. cannon, a sergeant, 25 privates, and 2 band musicians.

When Chief Man Afraid and his delegation saw this column cross the Laramie and head toward the Indian encampment about 2 p.m., with Lt. Grattan and Lucian Auguste, a half-breed interpreter much hated by the Indians, at its head, they were disturbed and decided to trail along. What they observed was not reassuring. The interpreter was obviously drunk, and at least some of the soldiers were nipping from a bottle of their own.

The first stop was at the Gratiot Houses storeroom, where Lt. Grattan told the clerks and few soldiers on guard about his mission, while interpreter Auguste galloped his horse among the Indians outside, shouting insults and brandishing his pistol. As they came to each band of Indians, Grattan issued orders for them to stay in camp, which Auguste passed on, embellished with more threats and insults.

The next stop was at the Bordeaux Trading Post, hard by the main encampment, where Grattan told James Bordeaux to send for Conquering Bear. While they awaited his arrival, Auguste continued his campaign of insults and threats among the Indians in the area. Bordeaux, who understood the Sioux language as well as English, was greatly alarmed and told Grattan the man [Auguste] had to be stopped or trouble was sure to follow. He also told the lieutenant if he would put Auguste inside the post away from the Indians that he, Bordeaux, could settle the whole thing in 30 minutes. Grattan took no action.

When Conquering Bear arrived, Grattan demanded that he surrender High Forehead. The Bear told him High Forehead was not a member of his tribe, merely a visitor at his camp, and he had no authority over him or to surrender him. The Brule chief also increased his offer of indemnity to several ponies, and Bordeaux and other white men present all urged Grattan to delay further action until the Indian Agent arrived.

Lt. Grattan's answer was to march his men right into the Brule camp, point his cannon at Conquering Bear's lodge, line his men up on both sides, order them to cap their rifles and be ready to fire. He then stepped forward and told the Brule chief he intended to personally search the camp and arrest his man. Bear said that would be a bad thing to do, and offered a mule, worth at least two horses, in addition to the ponies --- many times the value of any cow. The pow-wow continued. Auguste's inter-preting became more inaccurate and insulting to both sides. Then suddenly High Forehead stepped from one of the lodges, shouted that he would not surrender but was not afraid to die, and was ready to fight Grattan to the death.

Meanwhile, from the roof of his trading post, Bordeaux and several other white men could see that braves from the other tribes had quietly surrounded Grattan on both flanks and the rear. They persuaded Bordeaux to go and replace Auguste as interpreter to prevent a fight. Bordeaux jumped on his horse and started, but he was too late.

Several scattering shots were fired and one Indian fell. The Bear shouted at his Brules to hold their fire, that maybe the white men would go away. Instead, Grattan stepped back into line, grabbed the lanyard of one cannon, and signaled his men to fire. The cannon were pointed a little too high and their balls whistled harmlessly over the tepees, but at the first volley Conquering Bear, who had tried so hard to prevent a clash, fell mortally wounded.

The Brules, gathered about their fallen chieftain, responded with a flight of arrows. Lt. Grattan was one of the first to go down --- his body carried 24 arrows when recovered. The interpreter and a soldier holding Grattan's horse galloped off toward the Holy Road at the first shot and were next to be killed. Several men piled into the wagon and the driver whipped his horses back over the trail. Indians covering the rear took care of them. The remaining 15 or 20 soldiers retreated over rough ground to the base of a brush-covered hill and, for a time, their fire held most of the warriors beyond arrow range. But when they made a dash from their cover across a flat stretch toward the Holy Road, hundreds of mounted warriors charged and hacked them down. Within a few hours after those thirty men had left Fort Laramie, full of high spirits in more ways than one, all were dead.

The now thoroughly-enraged warriors spared Bordeaux and his family because he was a brother-in-law of the tribe and long-time friend, and the Brules failed to find the several white men hidden on his roof. But they rampaged through the night, swearing death to all whites. Next morning they rode up-river to the warehouse where their goods were stored --- and from which the few soldiers and clerks had discreetly retired --- helped themselves to what they wanted and scattered most of the goods --- flour, sugar, bacon, etc. --- from the shelves in a fury of destruction. Then on they went to Fort Laramie, where some say they made a token attack, others that they contented themselves with circling the Fort on their ponies and driving off all loose stock. On the third day, they struck their great camp on the Platte and returned to their various hunting grounds.

So it was not until the fourth day that a civilian and military burial party was able to reach the scene of the massacre. What they found was not pretty. The slain had been mutilated beyond recognition. Hot August sunshine had done the rest. Only the body of Lt. Grattan was returned to the post for burial. It was identified by a watch he was carrying. The rest were quickly covered in one common, shallow grave. The incident triggered a quarter-century of intermittent savage warfare on the plains.

About 1920, John Hunton showed the writer this common grave. It was a depression about 15 feet in diameter and perhaps 3 feet deep in the center. The surrounding land was still brush-covered river bottom. He told us it had been a mound when he first came to the country in 1867. The winds of more than half a century had hollowed it out. Mr. Hunton stepped into the depression and scratched around with his cane. He unearthed a tarnished brass button, a uniform collar insignia, and what appeared to be a piece of arm bone and a human tooth. We reburied these evidences of an ancient tragedy in the dusty earth and went away from there.

An Ill-fated Trek to Washington

Tues, Mar 23 [1875] --- Expedition under Capt. Mix started to bring miners out of Black Hills . . . Considerable excitement about Blk. Hills . . .

The above long-past and forgotten minor military movement was a prelude to major war with the Sioux, which was to follow discovery of gold in the Black Hills of South Dakota and the rush of thousands of miners into that area, which the Indians considered a violation of their territory and of their peace treaties with the white man.

It is difficult to imagine the magnitude of this mass migration from all over the nation --- men lured by the magic word "gold", with their dreams of quick and easy wealth, and the women who always follow the path of such adventurers. Newspaper stories and other records of the day show that before the rush was over, large organized groups from the states of Maine, Connecticut, Wisconsin, Missouri, Michigan, Pennsylvania, Virginia, Illinois, Tennessee, Louisiana, and New York --- to mention a few --- flooded into Cheyenne, all clawing their way toward that Promised Land. Hunton's entries in his diaries for that "feverish period" indicate that 4-horse and 6-horse coaches were passing through Bordeaux at all hours of the day and night.

The Chinese whom Hunton mentions more than once as being among the throngs which passed through Bordeaux for the Black Hills were apparently not all lured by dreams of raw gold, as were most of their white brethren. Some seemed to have in mind the turning of an honest penny by the neat trick of trying to keep those miners clean. At least two of these gentlemen, Al Hong and Hong Lee by name, are recorded as striking out for the "Hills" with complete laundry outfits.

[At first, the Sioux used peaceful means in trying to persuade the white man to honor the treaties and stem the flow of gold-crazed miners, as discussed below.]

> *Fri, May 7 [1875] --- Louis Loab passed,*
> *said Indians were on way to Washington.*
> *Sat, May 8 --- Making fence. Indians*
> *passed going to Washington . . .*

The above laconic entries were the prelude to considerable history. We are indebted to the Hon. Joseph C. O'Mahoney, chairman of the Senate Committee on Indian Affairs, the Library of Congress, the Annual Reports of the Commissioner of Indian Affairs for the years 1874 - 1877, and the *Washington Star* for much of the following information concerning that delegation of Indian chieftains who passed through Hunton's Road Ranch at Bordeaux that May day on their way to see the Great White Father in Washington.

They were headed by Chief Red Cloud.

This ancient photograph, identified as Red Cloud in Mr. Hunton's writing, was carefully preserved among his papers, together with the photographs of other Indians, all identical in size and mounting, which Mr. Hunton likewise identifies as

Black Crow, Iron Shell, White Eyes, No Flesh, and Mr. and Mrs. Thigh. These photographs presumably are mementos they brought home with them (and apparently just about the only thing they did bring home with them) from that ill-fated trip. Printing on the back proclaims they were all taken by "Alex Gardner, [one of the most famous photographers of that era], 921 Penna. Ave., Washington, D. C."

Others in Red Cloud's delegation, according to Washington records, were American Horse, Little Wound, Shoulder, Conquering Bear [not to be confused with the chief Conquering Bear who was killed during the Grattan fiasco described above], Face Sitting Bull, Trail Lance, East Thunder, Black Bear, Iron Horse, Pawnee Killer, and Mr. and Mrs. Bad Wound. In all there were three delegations from the Sioux Nations which converged on Washington that spring, the other two being led by Lone Horn, chief of the Minneconjous, and Chief Spotted Tail.

Three Indian Agents, Maj. H. W. Bingham, J. J. Saville, and E. A. Howard accompanied the delegations, and William Garnett and Louis Bordeaux went along as interpreters. They arrived in Washington on the 16th and 17th of May and were quartered at the Tremont House.

Chief Red Cloud and the delegations first met President Grant at the White House on May 19th, but after greeting them, the President said he was too busy to discuss their problems that day and shunted them along to talk with the Commissioner of Indian Affairs and the Secretary of the Interior --- a real case of "passing the Buck" if there ever was one.

This brush-off seemed to annoy the big chiefs. Lone Horn is reported to have "informed the President that he and his forefathers had owned all of this country at one time, and that he was claiming entire ownership, as of that day, for the Indians", and they were "fully prepared to fight for their rights". Next Spotted Tail and Red Cloud chimed in and said, "with angry gestures that unless he appointed a day very soon to meet with them, he, the President, would be sorry". But Grant, it seems, just wasn't in any mood for pow-wowing and "with this the entire delegation marched out".

At a subsequent meeting with the Indian Commissioner, "Red Cloud spoke first, maintaining that the white man had told him many lies, and he had come to Washington to find the truth from 'The Great White Father' ". He received a promise that they could see the President some other day.

On May 21st, "the delegation and their interpreters appeared at the Commissioner's office to demand a change of quarters from the Tremont House to the Washington House, maintaining that their rooms were too small". The Commissioner's long reply to this complaint added up to "no soap", and the Indians went away mad again. At one conference, Lone Horn complained "they did not have enough food on their reservation nor weapons with which to obtain food". The Commissioner's come-back was that Lone Horn's band was short of food because they "entertained and supported other Indians" --- and the request for guns was turned down because "Bad Indians" might get them. It is not surprising that the boys began to feel they were getting no place fast. On one of these occasions, the Commissioner asked Spotted Tail how he felt about the situation, and the chief replied, "I don't brag about the Black Hills country when I am talking to white men, but I love it and don't want to leave."

Finally, on May 26th, they got their interview with President Grant, and the old general lost no time in laying down the law of might makes right. He is quoted in part as saying: "They must see that the white people outnumber the Indians two hundred to one in the territories of the United States. This number is increasing rapidly and before many years, it will be impossible to fix the limits where the Indians can prevent the white people from going. It will soon become necessary for white people to go to countries, whether occupied by Indians or not, the same as they go from one state to another."

And so Red Cloud and his red Brothers got the truth from their "Great White Father". The President then proceeded to " . . . point out to them the advantages both to themselves and their children if they enter into an agreement I shall propose to them. There is a territory south of where they now live, where game and grass is better, and where whites can be sent among them to teach them the arts of civilization. This year there has been great difficulty in keeping the white people from the Black Hills in search of gold . . . Each recurring year this same difficulty will be encountered unless the right to go to that country is granted by the Indians. In the end, this purpose to get into that country may lead to hostilities between the whites and the Indians without any special faults on either side." President Grant then ended the interview by saying, "I want the Indians to think of what I have said to them. I don't want them to talk today, but to speak freely with the Secretary of the Interior and the Commissioner of Indian Affairs."

They met with Secretary of the Interior Delano and Commissioner Smith on May 27th and were given some more blunt advice. After telling them how good it was for the Indians to be at peace with the whites and pointing out that the government was spending $1,200,000 annually on supplies for the Sioux, the Secretary threatened discontinuance of further aid unless they accepted the government's offer, being quoted as saying, "Now if you don't do what is right, Congress will refuse to give you any more aid." (That still seems to have a familiar echo in some of today's official statements concerning our foreign policy).

And what was the government's offer for the Black Hills and other concessions? "Commissioner Smith then stated that Congress would give them $25,000 for their land and send them into Indian Territory to settle." No, friend, we didn't leave off any ciphers. $25,000 was the government's offer. Spotted Tail's reply to Secretary Delano's proposition was something of an oration, its logic worthy, in our opinion, of preservation and was as follows.

> "My father, I have considered all the Great Father told me, and have come here to give you an answer . . . When I was here before, the President gave me my country, and I put my stake down in a good place, and there I want to stay . . . I respect the Treaty (doubtless referring to the Treaty of 1868) but the white men who come in our country do not. You speak of another country, but it is not my country; it does not concern me, and I want nothing to do with it. I was not born there . . . If it is such a good country, you ought to send the white men now in our country there and let us alone . . . "

Wrangling continued on a number of minor points, including interpretation of the terms of the Treaty of 1868, but the Indians refused to sign any new treaty or agreement until they had returned home to consult with their people. The delegations left Washington empty-handed on June 4th.

Had a successful solution been found, the great Indian wars of 1876 might not have been fought, and there would have been no Custer Massacre. For a time, our government did try, unsuccessfully, to stop the tide, according to most historians --- but the magic word "Gold" was too powerful a drug, then as now. In vain did Washington issue its proclamations. In vain did our troops try to block the trails, but in retrospect, perhaps no human power could have stemmed that ant-like, gold-crazed horde.

So the Indians fought and thousands died. But their cause was hopeless. The strength of the Sioux was broken. President Grant "spoke with a straight tongue" --- the odds were too great. [Dim and distant echoes from those savage wars are recorded in the following section].

- Subduing the Sioux -
The Bloody Wars of 1876

[At the beginning of 1876], the gold rush to the Black Hills and Indian resentment at this "invasion" were mounting like thunderheads on opposite sides of the horizon, soon to meet head on. The following stories of the day [from publications such as the *Cheyenne Leader* and the *Omaha Bee*] give some idea of the white man's feelings and viewpoint, but not, of course, of the red man's, who had no newspapers to speak for him.

"Jan. 1, 1876 --- (Red Cloud Agency). Indian Agent Hastings yesterday issued an order for all squaw men and gamblers and roustabouts and all others who are not in the pay of the government or the store keepers, to leave the reservation within 48 hours or abide the consequences, which are . . . [to be evacuated] by the military . . . This created much 'fancydancing' all around here tonight . . . Most of the floating population talk of starting for the Black Hills."

"Jan. 1, 1876 --- Capt. James Gillis, Quartermaster of the U. S. Army at Cheyenne Depot, has put a considerable force at work rebuilding the telegraph line from here to Fort Laramie . . . Now that the miners are leaving here every week by the hundreds for the gold regions of the Black Hills, it will soon be necessary to have telegraphic communication with that country."

"Jan. 5, 1876 --- (Dispatch from Fort Laramie). Miners here for supplies report a party from the Missouri River arriving in the Hills, worn out from fighting Indians on their long journey . . . The Sioux do not disturb travel on the routes to the Black Hills from this place [Fort Laramie] . . . Allen and his Varieties have arrived in the Hills."

"Jan. 8, 1876 --- The opening of the Black Hills to the occupancy of that country by the civilized race is now an assured fact. Whether the indolent savages who claim the Black Hills as their heritage shall peacefully consent . . . or forcibly resist . . . the tide that has set in can never be turned back."

The flood gates were now open, and that northbound trek to "The Hills" was on in earnest. Wyoming's rugged winter, nor Sun Dogs in the sky, nor furious savages here below, could longer hold in check that white stampede for gold. It was also a boon to the travel business, Wyoming's first tourist cavalcade. Some idea of the transportation, supplies, and accommodations provided may be gathered from these Cheyenne news stories of January 22, 1876.

"Mr. George W. Homan, Jr. of Omaha has arrived in Cheyenne to look after the interests of the proposed Black Hills stage line. He is not entirely satisfied that his way stations would be safe from the incursions of the Sioux . . . But with troops at Spotted Tail and Red Cloud [Agencies] to prevent any flank movement or outbreak of the only Indians who can do any harm, we would consider the new stage route as safe as the route from here to Omaha."

"J. W. Deer of Red Cloud Agency has established ranches along the route from Fort Laramie to the Black Hills at convenient distances and will keep accommodations for miners . . . the first at Government Farm, 15 miles from Fort Laramie. The next is on the headwaters of Running Water, 20 miles further, the next on Old Woman's Fork of the Cheyenne River, and the last on Cheyenne River a day and a half from Custer."

"John S. Collins, energetic Post Trader at Fort Laramie, has recently shipped through E. Nagle, of Cheyenne, an immense amount of flour, bacon, and other provisions for . . . supplying miners in the Black Hills. Fort Laramie is only 130 miles from the Hills, is the nearest telegraph station, and the nearest mail station except for [the] Red Cloud [Agency]."

But while these and commonplace activities were being pursued in a tranquil way in the vicinity of Fort Laramie, war and personal tragedy (as frequently happens) were creeping up inexorably on the Huntons and many others --- indicating once again how fortunate it probably is that few of us have prophetic vision. [This was a newspaper story of January 29, 1876 in Cheyenne.]

"(Dispatch from Fort Pease on the Yellowstone) Sitting Bull's band of Sioux attacked a party near Fort Pease, killing one man and wounding five others. Another party of nine men are cut off from the Fort by the Indians, who number several hundred. It is feared that the entire garrison will be massacred unless speedily assisted."

With war with the Sioux having reached that "inevitable" stage, editors of the day were inspired to wax patriotic, propagandish, and almost poetic. The *Laramie Sentinel* painted the picture as follows.

" MILITARY PREPARING FOR OUTBREAK "

"Miners In No Danger If Well Armed and Watchful"

"Feb. 18, 1876: Orders were received yesterday at Fort Sanders (an early military post near the city of Laramie) to have the cavalry horses all shod and extra sets of shoes fitted to each horse. All the pack animals were started for Fort Russell (now the Warren Air Base adjoining Cheyenne) and two cavalry companies here are ordered to hold themselves in instant readiness to leave at a moment's notice. A force of 12 or 15 companies of cavalry will, within three weeks, go into the northern country and rendezvous in the very midst of the Sioux.

"General [George] Crook expects an outbreak and is preparing for it. Miners should not start in parties of less than 10, and should be well-armed and watchful. With these precautions, there is . . . no danger . . . To put off an aggressive campaign against the Sioux would be simply foolishness . . . The Indians would scatter all over northern Wyoming if left until April or May, and it would then take a larger army than Uncle Sam can command to force them back to the Missouri River.

"Our people will rejoice to see 'our boys in blue' march to the front in order to remove the ravaging and murdering savages from a territory which is destined to be the garden spot and treasure house of this republic."

[John Hunton witnessed some of the military activity at that time from his headquarters at Bordeaux, as indicated by the following entries in his 1876 diary.]

Wed, Feb 23 --- At Ranch all day fixing harness. Gen. Crook passed.

Thurs, Feb 24 --- Lt. Reynolds & Mr. Moore here last night and two miners from the Hills who report very unfavorable. Gen. Reynolds passed to (Fort) Laramie. Five Companies 3rd Cavalry passed going to Fetterman. Wagons and pack trains with them all want hay. I think they are going to try to recover stolen stock from Indians and to force them to go on reservation, and will establish camp near old Ft. Reno. Ranger Jones passed with some horses recovered from Indians.

And the *Cheyenne Leader* reports General Crook is ready for action, but not fooling himself about the job ahead.

"Feb. 26, 1876: A *Leader* reporter interviewed General Crook yesterday. The General leaves for Fort Laramie this morning at 8:00 accompanied by his aide, Lt. Bourke . . . Once at Fort Laramie . . . the General will take the field on horseback and personally superintend the campaign against the Redskins. No aggressive movement will be made until the Indians begin their outbreak, an event liable to occur any moment.

"The General apprehends that the work of the campaign will be unusually arduous, owing to the fact that the soldiers under him are completely unaccustomed to Indian fighting.

"Yesterday, he (General Crook) spent an hour in the telegraph office here in correspondence with General Grant, General Sherman, Lt. General Sheridan, General Custer, and the commanders of Forts Laramie, Fetterman, and Lincoln."

By now the gold excitement, that lure of quick, easy wealth, was mushrooming from the Black Hills in all directions like an atomic cloud. [But the shadow of the Sioux hung over all, as indicated by this newspaper excerpt.]

"March 11, 1876: Sitting Bull . . . has collected 1,500 braves at the mouth of the Powder River in the Yellowstone country and defies the combined forces of Generals Custer and Crook, numbering 2,000 men . . . An expedition is already enroute for the neighborhood of the obstinate redskins . . . "

[As mentioned in chapter 1 and further supported by the first diary entry below], all of this military preparation isn't hurting John Hunton, at least not in the pocketbook, he being a "war contractor" of that day.

*Sun, Mar 12 [1876] --- Went to Post
(Fetterman) in wagon. Rec'd voucher from*

Capt. Gillis for $2662.77, signed and returned it.

Thurs, Mar 23 --- Jack Russell & Tom Reed got in from Crook's expedition and reported its failure.

Sun, Mar 26 --- Went to Post (Fetterman). Expedition arrived. Made a disastrous campaign. Lost many mules and horses . . . Indians retained possession of battlefield and the dead, & recaptured all their ponies, 700 in all. Much hardship endured by troops . . .

Crook's ignominious affair with Crazy Horse's band, forcing him to return to Fetterman and reorganize for a summer campaign, left our military glum and red-faced. While the military brass cast about for scapegoats on which to hang the blanket of humiliation received from Crazy Horse, our boys in blue sought solace in alcohol, as soldiers are frequently wont to do whether in victory, in defeat, or in between.

[In May, 1876], while Hunton was quietly nursing his shock [at the murder of his brother, Jim] with the medicine of his work and life's daily routine, word of the mounting hazards and apparent panic on that "safe" route [from Fort Laramie] to the Black Hills began to spread. [The *Cheyenne Leader* gave this report, which undoubtedly fueled the bonfire of fear.]

> "Those (Indians) who escaped the attack on Crazy Horse's village on March 17th have joined him. Sitting Bull, Bull Eagle, and other hostile chiefs are doing their utmost to persuade the young men to leave all the reservations. The Indians are getting large amounts of ammunition by half-breeds.

"Gen. Crook's expedition will start out May 15. It will be divided into three detachments, moving from the Union Pacific, from Fort Ellis down the Yellowstone and from Fort Lincoln up the Yellowstone.

"Another effort is about to be made to pacify the gentle savages about the invasion of the Black Hills. A new peace commission will start for Red Cloud Agency to induce Red Cloud, Spotted Tail, and company to abandon their present camping grounds and take up new quarters on the upper Missouri. One commissioner, C. P. Beauvais of St. Louis, lived among the Sioux for many years."

Fri, May 26 [1876] --- Expedition making much preparation to leave.

All men, teams, and supplies of this large expedition of 15 cavalry companies and five infantry companies Crook was assembling at Fetterman to move against the Sioux had to be ferried across the swollen Platte on a cable-boat for their march to the north, and the job of ferrying was a real one. In those days, long before the great dams which now store and control the waters of the Platte were even thought of, that stream in springtime was indeed a mighty river.

[At the same time, the press gave the following details about an approach that was proposed to help curb hostilities.]

"May 27, 1876: Gen. William Vandever, U. S. Indian Inspector, wired Secretary of Interior on May 24. 'If the Military can be restrained to [only] protecting settlers in the Black Hills and guarding the routes, the trouble will soon cease. Aggressive

movements tend to incite the Sioux to war. Spotted
Tail and Red Cloud want peace. They will accept
fair terms and use their influence to bring others in."

But Vandever's advice was not followed, and peace was not to
be.

>   *Sun, June 25 --- Heard of Crook's fight*
> *on the 17th inst . . .*

The "Crook's fight on the 17th inst" to which Hunton refers
above was the battle on the Rosebud River, tributary to the
Yellowstone, where Crook, with his Crow and Shoshone allies,
met Crazy Horse at the head of some 6,000 Sioux and Cheyenne
warriors. General Crook's aide, Lt. Bourke, credits our troops
with a win, but some authorities give the decision to Crazy
Horse, who retired from the field with his dead and wounded
while our forces likewise drew back to their wagon trains.
General Crook's horse was shot from under him during the
engagement. Not being there, we offer no opinion as to who
won. Perhaps it was a draw.

>   *Fri, July 7 [1876] --- Custer Massacre*
> *confirmed . . .*

Mr. Hunton does not seem to have been overcome with
emotion by the Custer Massacre. It was not closely connected
with his immediate daily life and business world. But for most
Americans, that event became the best-known and most firmly
fixed episode of western Indian warfare. Perhaps that was due in
considerable measure to the advertising enterprise of one of the
nation's leading brewery concerns of that day which took the
purely imaginative and highly dramatic painting of "Custer's Last

Stand" and made huge reprints of it, which were framed and hung in most American saloons. After a given number of drinks with that exciting and gory piece of art confronting one across the bar, the impression was apt to be deep and lasting. It must have sold a lot of beer.

> *Sat, July 15 --- Crook . . . on Goose Creek inactive. Indians in large numbers hovering near him . . . Fifth Cavalry to reinforce Crook . . .*
>
> *Wed, July 19 --- 8 P.M. heard that 5th Cavalry had forced Indians who had left Red Cloud Agency to return to it. Heard that Bill Cody (Buffalo Bill) killed two Indians.*
>
> *Tues, July 25 --- Rec'd orders to kill beef for [General] Merritt . . .*

History records that General Merritt was on his way with ten companies of the Fifth Cavalry, 76 recruits for the 2nd and 3rd regiments, 60 extra horses, and a supply of ammunition to reinforce General Crook. Their forces joined on Goose Creek.

> *Tues, Aug 8 --- 100 Indians reported going toward Chug from Agencies. Courier arrived [at Fort Fetterman] from Crook . . . Crook's command were to start after Indians on 5th.*
>
> *Sat, Aug 12 --- Indians chased soldiers into Swan's Ranch, large party of Indians reported.*
>
> *Mon, Aug 21 --- Companies of 14th [Infantry] arrived at Fort Laramie.*

Tues, Sept 5 --- Cavalry and Infantry recruits passed for 4th Cav. and 9th Infty.
Sat, Sept 16 --- Gen. Sheridan passed...
Sun, Sept 17 --- Heard Crook had fight and killed few Indians...
Fri, Oct 27 --- Went to Post [Fort Laramie], heard [Crook's] expedition was coming here...
Sun, Nov 5 --- Gen. Crook & expedition left Fort Laramie today for Fetterman...
Tues, Nov 14 --- Expedition started at 10:00 A.M. [from Fort Fetterman]...

The above expedition, Crook's third and last major campaign in the area, was the one which finally succeeded in breaking the back of the desperate and often gallant resistance of the Cheyenne, Sioux, and other lesser tribes to the white man's invasion of the Black Hills and their ancestral hunting grounds. This time Crook's forces were more experienced in Indian warfare, far better supplied and equipped, and had the invaluable assistance of traitors --- large numbers of Indian scouts who, realizing the hopelessness of it all, deserted their embattled fellow tribesmen and came over to the whites.

After this campaign, there was still considerable "Indian trouble" for quite some time from a few desperate, fugitive bands who refused to give up. But one by one, the proud war chiefs came into the reservations in abject surrender, bringing their young fighting men with them, and were disarmed. The sun was fast setting for the Red Man in the West.

[Here's a final recollection about Crook's expeditions from one of John Hunton's narratives published in my grandfather's *Fort Laramie Scout.*]

"When General Crook's expedition went out about the last of May, I gave the General and his officers quite a quantity of dried elk meat. The General appreciated it very much, and told me a number of times that he never enjoyed anything more than to be able to put his hand in his coat pocket while on the march after Indians that summer, and pull out a piece of dried elk meat and munch away on it while the others were glad to get mule or pony meat." [Rank apparently had its privileges then, as now, but perhaps to a lesser degree in frontier times.]

Crazy Horse - The Last Holdout

Tues, May 1 [1877] --- Heard that Crazy Horse and all his warriors were going into agency . . .

Crazy Horse, most fierce and implacable warrior of them all, and most skillful military strategist of the Sioux Nation, was the last of their great chiefs to surrender --- which he finally did with tongue in cheek. Even after he and his forces turned over their arms to the military at the Red Cloud Indian Agency, Crazy Horse still dreamed of a comeback, plotted to escape, kept the young braves he could influence in a state of foment, and encouraged their depredations. Because of these activities and his unbearable arrogance, General Crook finally ordered the personal arrest of Crazy Horse about September 1, 1877, causing the irrepressible old fighter to make his final futile break for freedom the night of September 3rd.

He managed to reach the Spotted Tail Agency, where he was taken into custody by fellow Indians more friendly to the white man, who brought him back to the Red Cloud Agency. While Crazy Horse was being placed in the guard house there, he suddenly drew a knife and attacked his captors. He was stabbed and bayoneted in the fracas and thus died, still fighting. [According to another article penned by John Hunton for the *Fort Laramie Scout*], the end of Crazy Horse also marked the end of Indian terror and stealing in the vicinity of Fort Laramie.

CHAPTER 3

HEROES, VILLAINS, AND THOSE IN BETWEEN

[My grandfather's books about Mr. Hunton and his diaries chronicled] the life and passing of a fascinating generation, a breed of men and women whose lives were often hard but seldom dull. Perhaps no other man knew that life better than John Hunton or recorded it in such careful detail. He also knew the men and women who made the history of his day, and they knew and respected him. [Episodes from some of their lives, and profiles of others, are presented in this chapter.]

Memories of "Calamity" and "Wild Bill"

Martha Jane [or Mary Jane] Canary is said to have been nicknamed "Calamity Jane" by an army man, Captain Eagan, for saving his life, after he had been wounded in an Indian fight, by killing one of the Indians and then placing the unconscious Eagan across her horse and riding with him to safety. The history of this remarkable woman is a many-sided and piecemeal thing, made up largely of stories and alleged incidents in her career --- many of them so conflicting as to be patently untrue. But certain things about her are clear. She was a profligate who prostituted her body but not her valor or compassion and kindness to others in sickness or need. She was an unusual combination of those human characteristics which men arbitrarily label "good" and "bad". This sharp contrast in her makeup between the best and the worst qualities inherent in all mankind have made her a legendary frontier figure.

The following is what Mr. Hunton had to say concerning that uninhibited lady [shown below in an 1895 photograph] and his summation of her adventurous career, as written for and published in the *Fort Laramie Scout* shortly before his death.

"About the time of the first appearance of Calamity Jane in this part of the country (meaning the Fort Laramie area), in the fall of 1873, Ecoffey and Cuny started a large trading outfit [three miles] west of Fort Laramie on the north side of the Laramie River, where they carried on quite an extensive business selling goods, running a saloon and general road ranch.

"In 1874, business got very slack with them, and they decided to add new attractions, and for that purpose they constructed eight two-room cottages to be occupied by women. They sent to Omaha, Kansas City, and other places and in a short time had their houses occupied by ten or more young women, all of whom were known as sporting characters.

"Among this bunch was 'Calamity Jane', who was of the type generally given her by magazine writers and newspaper correspondents. Her achievements have been very greatly magnified by every writer I have ever read, for she was among the commonest of her class. She seldom ever carried a rifle when riding horseback from place to place, and I do not think I ever saw her with both rifle and pistol. Her one redeeming trait was that she seldom spoke of what she had done or could do with gun or pistol. I have no recollection of ever seeing her shoot at any object, but I have seen her fire her pistol into space.

"I am not sure when I first saw her, but I think it was in 1875 . . . At that time, my house was at Bordeaux, 27 miles from Fort Laramie on the Cheyenne road. My ranch was a general road ranch and place of entertainment for the traveling public, which gave me a good opportunity to see and hear all that was going on. Jane often stopped at my place, especially during the years of 1876, 1877, and 1878, while the Cheyenne and Black Hills stage coaches were in full swing.

"She went out with the Dodge expedition in 1875 and remained with the expedition until detected, when she was ordered to remain with the wagon train until the train returned to Fort Laramie . . . The wagon master, old Jim Duncan, demurred at the order, but saw to it that she went back to Fort Laramie.

"She then resumed her old life at the Cuny and [Ecoffey] ranch and other places of similar character at Fort Laramie and Fort Fetterman until the organization of General Crook's army in May, 1876, when she and three other women of the same character were smuggled out with the command and remained with it until found out and ordered back.

"After the battle of Rose Bud, in June 1876, Crook's army lay idle on Goose Creek and Tongue Rivers until joined by General Merritt . . . Soon after, General Crook ordered his extra wagons to be sent back to Fort Fetterman with the sick and wounded, and I know Calamity Jane was with it, for I saw her on the way up to John Brown Ranch the same day the train arrived in Fetterman. She soon left Fetterman, and I do not think returned there that year, but she was in Fetterman in the spring of the year 1877 for a short time."

The final paragraphs of Mr. Hunton's article on Calamity Jane bring in "Wild Bill" (Hickok) . . . as follows.

"I will now refer to . . . 'Wild Bill', whom I knew fairly well in 1874 and late in the year 1875, when he was making his home in Cheyenne. During that time, I do not think he knew 'Calamity Jane' . . .

"On June 30, 1876, 'Bill' and a party of men who were on their way to the Black Hills mines, traveling with a four-horse team and wagon, camped about two miles south of my ranch. The next morning they passed my place and 'Bill' stopped long enough to say 'How'. He then said, 'So long, Jack' and went away. ('Jack' is the nickname by which Hunton was known in the early days.) A few hours afterward, Waddie S. Bacom, one of my men, came in and said, 'Mr. Hunton, I met a man down the road who said he was 'Wild Bill' and wanted you to go to the place he camped last night and get his cane, which he stuck in the ground at his head where he made his bed last night in the edge of a patch of bushes, and send it to him at Deadwood by someone you can trust to deliver it to him. Be sure not to send it except by some mutual friend whom you both know, as he did not want to take any chance of losing it.' I sent the man for the cane, and he brought it to me.

"In less than a month, I heard of Bill's death. (He was assassinated at Deadwood by a stage driver, Jack McCall, who some say was threatened with lynching for the deed by a mob reputedly led by 'Calamity Jane'.) [But] . . . at the time of Bill's death, Jane was in the hands of the military authorities.

"I kept the cane until 1921 and then gave it to Miss Eunice G. Anderson, State Historian, to be deposited in the museum of the Wyoming Historical Society, where it is now deposited and can be seen."

A newspaper story of that day told how Calamity Jane once took Mr. James C. Abney, who operated the first scheduled stage and mail line between Cheyenne and Fort Laramie, "for a ride" in one of his own rigs, figuratively speaking. On June 10, 1876, this redoubtable frontier lass rented a horse and buggy from Abney's livery to drive out to Fort Russell and back. Fort Russell was only a mile or so from Cheyenne, but Calamity became so preoccupied with her bottle that she went right by it without noticing and continued on her merry way throughout the night until she reached Chugwater, fifty miles further north.

Next morning she must have been hangoverishly suspicious that Fort Russell had moved, but doggedly kept searching until she came to Fort Laramie, ninety miles from where she started. Apparently deciding that Fort Laramie offered opportunities for both business and pleasure which were at least worth looking into, she parked her buggy, turned old dobbin loose to graze, and proceeded to make herself at home. Some days later, one Joe Rankin arrived from Cheyenne, retrieved Mr. Abney's property, and left Mistress Calamity peacefully to her own affairs, which are understood to have been many and varied.

[This story seemingly explains how Calamity was in the right neighborhood for sneaking into General Crook's camp and returning to Fort Fetterman with his sick and wounded soldiers, as recorded above by John Hunton. Perhaps she tagged along with General Merritt and his troops that July when they marched to reinforce Crook.]

[On March 17, 1887, the *Cheyenne Leader* reported:]

" . . . After an absence of 10 or 11 years, the notorious Calamity Jane, who used to figure so prominently in police courts and sporting circles in this city, has again made her appearance here, but evidently in a very dilapidated condition, according to those who have seen her . . . Calamity has had a checkered career, and has for years been known not only here but in Deadwood and many other towns in the far west . . . "

Pioneer Russell Thorp, of Cheyenne, sent [my grandfather] this account of Calamity's last days and burial at Deadwood, South Dakota.

"In her old age, Jane was destitute and returned to the Black Hills. Sam Tillitt, whom I knew very well, was a railroad engineer between Edgemont and Deadwood. He discovered Jane on his train, made her comfortable, and arranged for her care at Central City, a few miles from Deadwood . . . Not long after that she died.

"A few leading citizens of Deadwood were gathered in Mike Russell's saloon for their usual mid-afternoon drink when word of Jane's death reached them. They talked it over and decided to give her a big last sendoff in appreciation of what she did nursing miners through the smallpox epidemic.

The idea of making this a really memorable funeral grew and grew, with a few more drinks, and word was sent forth calling on all business houses to close during the services. Then came the question of where to dig her grave, and it was concluded as appropriate that she be buried in Mount Moriah Cemetery, alongside Wild Bill Hickok. Now Wild Bill had absolutely no use for Jane, but this distinguished, self-appointed committee decided it would be a good joke on the old boy to make him 'layup' with her for all eternity. I knew four of the men who planned the funeral [Albert Malter, Frank Ankeney, Jim Carson, and Anson Higby], and all of them told me the same story.

"Not long ago, here in Cheyenne, someone told me a fantastic story that Bill was married to Jane.

This is definitely not true, because the records in Cheyenne show that he was married to Agnes Lake, a circus horseback rider. After Hickok's death, she sold their race horse for eight hundred dollars and left Wyoming. She has not been heard from since."

The Saga of Fallen Leaf

[The military and emigrants' lust for land, gold, and adventure weren't the only forces that threatened the Sioux's way of life during this bygone era. For instance, some of them were lured from their tribes by a fascination for the "white man" and his culture. In his works, my grandfather presented the following case in point --- the sad story of an obsessed maiden, Fallen Leaf, and her father, Spotted Tail, whose "ill-fated" journey to Washington in 1875 with other chieftains and their delegations was previously described in chapter 2.]

The legend of Ah-ho-appa (Fallen Leaf) and of her father Shan-tag-alisk (Chief Spotted Tail of the Brule Sioux) has been often told in song and story, and in many ways. At least part of it is true. It is a strange tale of intermingled fact and fancy about a girl who wanted to live and love in a world of which she was not a part --- and of her father, who was a remarkable leader of men.

In the summer of 1928, a few months before his death, John Hunton was interviewed at Fort Laramie by Joseph G. Masters. He showed Mr. Masters where Ah-ho-appa had been buried on a scaffold and told him what he knew of the circumstances. Mr. Masters then wrote a newspaper feature story about her. In 1960, Russell Thorp of Cheyenne sent [my grandfather] a clipping of the story --- and photographs of the scaffolding that held her remains for many years [shown on the following page] and of her father.

Ah-ho-appa must have been a lonely girl, not in physical or spiritual harmony with her own people, or so the legend goes. Since she did not feel and think as they did, she could not be one with them. And from the whites, whom she admired and apparently wished to emulate, she was set apart by the chasms of heredity, skin color, and prejudice.

Thus it was that during a long visit at Fort Laramie about 1864, she would sit, day after day, alone and apart, on a bench at the Sutler's store, observing all that went on --- thinking who knows what thoughts and experiencing who knows what futile longings. Some stories say she was secretly in love with one of the dashing young officers. As to that, this writer has no evidence.

It is said the daily ceremony of guard mount always held her enthralled, and that the soldiers took pride in putting it on with special dash --- just for her. To them she was "The Princess", set apart by her grave reserve and dignity.

And then one day, Spotted Tail led his people north, back to the Powder River country, and took his daughter with him ---

away from Fort Laramie, which she never saw again in life. After her departure, at a gathering of officers at the old fort, one of them claimed to have known Ah-ho-appa in earlier years and said that even as a small girl, she had sworn never to marry an Indian, and she never did, although legend has it that some of the rich young braves of the tribe offered Shan-tag-alisk as many as 200 ponies for her hand. Another story is that on one occasion, a Blackfoot warrior attempted to carry her off by force and she cut him up with her knife to the point of death. Spotted Tail took such pride in this exploit that he never attempted to force her into marriage.

General Harney is said to have once presented her with a little red book which, although she could not read or even speak English, became one of her most treasured possessions. She dressed herself as a young man, liked to carry a gun like her father, and performed none of the squaws' menial tasks.

Two years after her departure from Fort Laramie found Ah-ho-appa dying in a lonely tepee on the Powder. Some said it was consumption --- others a broken heart. Shan-tag-alisk, in desperate grief, promised to take her back to Fort Laramie in the spring (1866), but Indian tradition, handed down from generation to generation, has it that she told her father how much she would love to go, but that it was too late.

And so she languished and died --- but not until after a promise from Spotted Tail that he would bury her on a hillside near Fort Laramie, where her spirit could look down upon the old parade ground and watch again the guard mount she loved so well. They wrapped the frail body in smoked deerskin and placed it upon two white ponies, lashed closely together, for the week-long journey through deep winter snows. A runner was sent ahead by Spotted Tail [shown in the following photograph mentioned earlier in this narrative], asking officers to grant his daughter's dying request for burial overlooking Fort Laramie.

The funeral cavalcade, while still some fifteen miles from the Fort, was met by a military escort sent by Post Commander Major George O'Brien. It consisted of an ambulance, a company of cavalry in dress uniform, and two 12-pound mountain howitzers. Ah-ho-appa's mortal remains were placed in the ambulance, her two white horses tied behind.

The entire garrison, headed by Col. Maynadier of the First U. S. Volunteers, turned out to meet the funeral cortege at the Platte River, about two miles from Fort Laramie. Next day the burial scaffold was erected on a gentle slope, half a mile or so north of the Fort hospital. It was made of stout poles, laced together at the top with thongs to hold the coffin. (About 1920, John Hunton took this writer to the site of that scaffold, some of which was still standing, with a few rotting boards from the coffin lying on the ground below.)

The two white ponies were sacrificed, their heads and tails nailed to the poles, so that Ah-ho-appa would not be afoot in the spirit world. The body, still in its deerskin shroud and further wrapped in a red blanket, was then placed in the elaborately-decorated coffin resting on a caisson and slowly hauled to the scaffold, escorted by the garrison in dress array.

Post Chaplain Wright conducted a formal white man's burial service. When he had finished, Spotted Tail indicated he wanted his daughter buried in the Indian way. He wanted to find her in the red man's happy hunting ground and be reunited with her there. He did not want her lost to him forever in the white man's heaven. His every wish was followed. When the ceremonies were over, Shan-tag-alisk cut what he doubtless hoped was the last thread binding his daughter to the white man's hereafter by returning to Chaplain Wright the parfleche sack containing the little army Episcopal prayer book given to her by General Harney many years before.

The soldiers were deployed in a large square about the scaffold. Within that square, the Indians stood in a circle around the coffin. Major O'Brien placed a pair of white kid cavalry gloves in the coffin to keep Fallen Leaf's hands warm on her lonely journey to the other world, and also a new dollar bill with which to buy food along the way. Then the Indian women came up, one by one, and talked to her in long, earnest whispers ---

doubtless messages for her to carry on to their own departed loved ones. And each put something she might need beside her body --- a bit of mirror, a string of beads, some little token. The lid was then fastened down, and the squaws lifted their princess to the top of the scaffold and lashed a buffalo skin over all, as the men stood by, mute and motionless. The soldiers, facing outward in their large square, fired a final salute of three volleys. Red men and white men then marched back together to the post as darkness fell and it began to sleet and snow --- that is, all marched back except the howitzer detail, which remained at the burial site, built a large fire, and discharged their cannon every half hour until daybreak. Sioux warriors apparently kept a watchful eye on the grave for quite some time after that.

Many years later, so the story goes, a young and impetuous military doctor came to Fort Laramie. He had the impudence and appalling lack of respect to remove the bones of Ah-ho-appa and make a skeleton of them for his office. One day, scouts brought word to the post that Shan-tag-alisk, with a party of warriors, was approaching to take away the remains of his child. Post authorities, in near panic, gave the great, friendly chief and his party a ceremonious welcome and persuaded him to rest over-night at the Fort before going to claim his daughter. This gave them a chance to replace Fallen Leaf's bones in her casket before morning and remove evidence that her grave had been violated. Had they failed, old Spotted Tail might have felt relieved of a promise he made to his daughter to never again make war on the whites --- and who could have blamed him? She was finally buried under a suitable monument at the Rosebud Agency in South Dakota.

Eugene Ware, an officer who was present and wrote an account of Fallen Leaf's burial at Fort Laramie, added this thought to his record.

"Her story is the story of the persistent melancholy of the human race; of kings born in hovels and dying there; of geniuses born where genius is a crime; of heroes born before their age and dying unsung; of beauty born where its gift was fatal; of mercy born among wolves; of statesmen born to find society not yet ripe for their labors to begin, and bidding the world adieu from the scaffold. The daughter of Shan-tag-alisk was one of those individuals found in all lands, at all places, and among all people; she was misplaced."

The record also indicates that her father was of unusual intellect with deep and abiding understanding of human rights and dignity, who realized the futility of war as an instrument of justice. If his reasoning and attitudes were those of an "ignorant savage", perhaps more of the same would be beneficial in high places --- even today.

- Six Mile Ranch -
A Favorite Spot for Killings

[In yet another *Fort Laramie Scout* article, John Hunton discussed some of the violent "white man" affairs which transpired in the neighborhood of Fort Laramie during his first eleven years there. His narrative indicated the following.]

"A great many tragedies . . . occurred in what is now Platte [and Goshen counties] during the eleven years, 1867-1877, inclusive, in which the Indians were constantly on the war path. But the Indians were not the only killers.

"The sequel to the killing of Baptiste Ladeau at Chug Springs [by Cy Williams and others, described in the 'Bordeaux - John Hunton's Home' section of chapter 1] was about as follows:

"In the spring and early summer of 1868, the government, having induced the Indians to consent to be moved to White Clay River, near Fort Russell on the Missouri River, had them concentrate into one large camp east of Fort Laramie about 8 miles, preparatory to starting about the latter part of May or the first of June. This mobilization included all white men with Indian families who cared to make the move.

"Cy Williams, having an Indian wife, abandoned Bordeaux late in March or early in April and moved to the Indian camp east of Fort Laramie so as to be ready to start with the Indians. After his wife had been interviewed by the relations of the murdered Ladeau boy, Williams was openly accused of the killing, which he denied, and was closely watched to see that he did not attempt to leave camp. This condition of affairs lasted about a week, when some half-breeds precipitated a gun fight. Williams was killed, but not before he had killed one half-breed, Charley Richards, and wounded two others, Joe Bissmetto and one whose name I have forgotten. Oliver P. Goodwin, an innocent spectator, was wounded, but not seriously."

[Mr. Hunton then wrote the ensuing passage in that article about an infamous place located between his home at Bordeaux and Fort Laramie.]

"The 'Six Mile' Ranch, [so named because it was
six miles from Fort Laramie], located on 'Baptist
Fork' on the Fort Laramie and Wheatland road in
what is now Goshen county, was a favorite place for
killing. The first man killed there was John Hunter,
the original owner, who was shot by 'Bud'
Thompson in October, 1868. The next two were
John Lowry and James McClosky, shot by John
Boyer in October, 1870. The next was Perry Arber,
a wood chopper who was assassinated by a man
whose name I have forgotten sometime in 1872 or
'73. Then followed two men at different times
during the Black Hills excitement prior to 1877.
   "The last one was Adolph Cuny, who was
assassinated by Clark Pelton, (one of the better-
known road agents of the day), in July, 1877 . . . "
(Pelton also went under the name of Billy Webster.
It happened shortly after Cuny had helped Deputy
Sheriff Hays of Fort Laramie place Pelton and a
fellow bandit, Dunc [or Dunk] Blackburn, under
arrest for a series of stage holdups a few weeks
earlier. After shooting Cuny, who died instantly, the
two desperadoes escaped and continued on their
merry criminal way for some time thereafter. But
Pelton was finally brought to trial, about two years
later, for Cuny's murder. He was convicted of man-
slaughter and got a light sentence.)

[Mr. Hunton didn't include an earlier Six Mile Ranch killing
in his article which also involved Dunk Blackburn, but he did
make the following reference to the incident, at least indirectly,
in his diary.]

Thurs, Nov 30 [1876] --- Cuny staid at Maxwell's last night on way to Cheyenne with Jules remains . . .

We are at a loss to explain why Mr. Hunton did not elaborate more in the above entry, but he may have had a good reason. Perhaps it was healthier in those days not to offer any opinion or comment, even in one's own diary, when famous bad men met and shot it out. But it is probably safe enough to speculate a little at this late date. "Jules remains" must have been all that was left of Jules Ecoffey, who was Cuny's partner in the road ranch of questionable repute [at which Calamity Jane made her first appearance in Wyoming Territory, as mentioned earlier in this chapter]. The story goes that Ecoffey was also a U. S. Marshal, [although this designation is questionable, according to my grandfather], and met his death at the hands of two widely if not favorably known road agents, Meyers and Dunk Blackburn, when they held up the Six Mile Ranch. That violent affair of long ago, [together with the other episodes recorded above], clearly demonstrates that the Six Mile Ranch was a tough "Hog Ranch", having plenty of whiskey and women --- plenty of fighting and murders, too.

A Time of Marauding Desperadoes

[As discussed in chapter 2], 1877 saw the end of Indian violence and marauding in the Fort Laramie area, according to John Hunton. However, his journal also indicates that white desperadoes and road agents [in addition to those identified in the last section] efficiently took over and carried on where the red man left off, [as highlighted by the following diary entries and narratives].

Wed, Sept 19 [1877] --- Got to Omaha.
[John Hunton was returning to Wyoming
from his Chicago business trip mentioned
in "The Rise and Fall of Fortune" section of
chapter 1.] Heard of [a Union Pacific] train
. . . being robbed at Big Springs last night.
Started to Cheyenne on U. P. train . . .

That U. P. train robbery at Big Springs, Nebraska, the night of September 18, 1877, was a big one. Masked men made off with an estimated $70,000 in money and other loot taken from the express car and passengers. In the mob there were such well-known stage coach robbers as Joel Collins, Sam Bass, Bill Heffridge, and Jim Berry, who was also suspected of being one of the gang which tried to hold up a stage coach near Deadwood the night of March 25, 1877, and killed the driver, Johnny Slaughter, putting 14 buckshot through his heart. Credit for the ultimate capture of these train robbers is given to U. S. Deputy Marshal M. F. Leach, of Ogallala, Nebraska. Mr. Hunton missed the exciting adventure by lingering just one day too long among the delights of Chicago.

Fri, Sept 27 [1878] --- Coach robbed last
night and one man killed, two wounded.

That holdup and cold-blooded killing is known in history as the Cold Springs stage robbery --- the last big "treasure coach" bandit-haul on the Cheyenne-Black Hills road. According to Luke Voorhees, operator of the line, it happened . . . like this.

About three o'clock on the afternoon of September 26th, the driver, H. E. Barnett, pulled up for a change of teams at a lonely log stable known as the Canyon Springs or Whisky Gap station near the present Wyoming-Dakota line about 35 miles south of

Deadwood. It was broad daylight. No danger was in sight --- but the stableman, William Miner, was not outside to meet them with a fresh six-horse team for the scheduled seven-minute change, as he should have been. Instead, he lay bound and gagged in a corner of the stable while five or six hard-eyed men lined the wall with their guns on the approaching stage through cracks between the logs from which the chinking had been removed.

Guard Hill, riding with the driver, jumped down to see why Miner was not out and ready with the new team. When he hit ground, the bandits opened fire. Hill fell, badly wounded. Guard Campbell was killed outright, and a third bullet grazed guard Smith's head, apparently knocking him cuckoo because for hours afterwards, he kept yelling that he was killed.

Chief Guard Davis left the coach from the side away from the barn, took his stand behind a large pine tree, and opened fire as the bandits came from the stable, wounding one or more and forcing the gang to take shelter behind the steel-lined coach. They called on Davis to surrender. He told them to go to hell. Then the leader of the mob, forcing terrified driver Barnett ahead of him as a shield, started advancing on Davis --- but he stopped about ten feet away when Davis said he would put a slug through both of them at the next step. After some parleying, they agreed to let Davis go his way if he would leave them with the coach.

The safe holding the rich cargo was guaranteed. The makers said it could not be opened with hand tools in less than twenty-four hours. So Davis backed off among the trees, keeping the bandits covered to protect himself from a bullet in the back until he was out of their sight --- then he hurried on foot for help to Beaver, the next station, some ten miles south. He made it in two hours.

With Davis gone, the outlaws made Barnett drive his stage off the road into the timber, lashed him to a wheel, and then proceeded to open the safe with a sledge hammer and cold chisels in less than an hour --- they apparently had not heard about that guarantee. The loot was divided and off they took through the wilderness in all directions.

The whole territory was aroused. Organized manhunts spread out, reaching into neighboring states and territories. The stage company offered a $2,500 reward. There were captures, bribes, escapes, confessions, and denials. Several suspects were lynched without ceremony. Others stood trial and were convicted on various counts. More than half of the loot was eventually recovered. But positive identification of all the men who stood behind that log stable wall and killed without even a rattlesnake's warning has never been established, to our knowledge. However, the resulting commotion did tend to discourage that sort of thing.

Sun, Dec 28 [1879] --- Am feeling quite
unwell. Dr. Crook prescribed for me . . .

About December, 1878, Dr. J. J. Crook of Cheyenne accompanied a *Sun* reporter to the sick bed of fabulous Lurline Monte Verdi, a strange and remarkable woman, to hear her statement of how she became a doctor and surgeon for the Charlie Ross gang of stage robbers.

Lurline had been married to an army physician and studied both medicine and surgery right along with him. But when her husband died, she took up a somewhat more exciting career --- she became a "Twenty-one" dealer and also a popular entertainer in the gambling halls of gold-crazy Deadwood. Soon she had an establishment of her own --- she called it a "restaurant" --- which apparently became a rendezvous for outlaws. The lady learned considerable about their business by keeping her ears open. She also kept on living by keeping her mouth shut.

One night Billy Mansfield (later hanged), whom Madam Monte Verdi called her "particular friend", made a date to meet her at a Deadwood opium smoking house where she was in the habit of spending "pleasant hours". When she showed up, Mansfield insisted that she accompany him to a deserted shack where McLaughlin and other members of the Ross gang were waiting for them. After swearing the lady to secrecy, they took her on to still another house where Johnny H. Brown (in jail at Cheyenne when she made her statement) had been lying delirious and without medical attention for some ten days, with a bullet in his side. She operated and he recovered, but the suspicious outlaws kept her under close surveillance and in fear for her life until the gang was broken up.

> *Wed, July 28 [1880] --- Arrived here [in*
> *Cheyenne] 10 A.M.   Getting Corlett to*
> *draw up the papers for Janis' place . . .*

The "Corlett" mentioned in the above entry was W. W. Corlett, an early Cheyenne lawyer who aided in the prosecution of bad man Charles Martin after Martin killed his partner in crime, one Mr. Jones, during a brawl. Previously, Martin and Jones were suspected of robbing General Dandy of $5,000. After being arrested for killing his sidekick, there being no jail in Cheyenne at that time, Martin is said to have been permitted to roam the streets of The Magic City, with a ball and chain attached to one leg. The desperado was not convicted and swore vengeance against his prosecutor when set at liberty. But the vigilantes took care of Mr. Martin before he could make good his threat.

John Hunton's Wide Circle of Friends

[Hundreds of John Hunton's contemporaries are mentioned in his diary entries. Narratives from my grandfather's works about a number of these people, besides those already discussed, with whom Mr. Hunton's journals indicate he had business and/or personal relationships --- and a few that I just find plain interesting --- are presented below.]

> *Fri, Dec 3 [1875] --- Started to [Fort]*
> *Fetterman . . . "Bat" with me.*

The "Bat" John Hunton is talking about was Baptiste "Little Bat" Garnier, [shown below in another photograph provided to my grandfather by Russell Thorp].

The following is a condensed history of Little Bat, as written by Mr. Hunton and published in the *Fort Laramie Scout.*

"Baptiste Garnier (Little Bat) was born in the neighborhood of Fort Laramie . . . in 1854. His father was a Canadian Frenchman, his mother a Sioux Indian, [and, as mentioned in chapter 1, his sister was Lallee, John Hunton's companion during his early years in Wyoming]. His father was killed by Cheyenne Indians in . . . 1856, at the mouth of Deer Creek where Glenrock now stands.

"When he was about eight years old, his mother having died, he was taken to the family of E. W. Whitcomb, whose wife was a relative. In 1872, he commenced making his home at my ranch at Bordeaux on Chugwater Creek . . . He developed into a fine worker . . . and an extraordinary fine huntsman . . .

"In March, 1876, he was (a guide) with the Crook expedition against the Sioux and was in the fight with Crazy Horse's band of Indians. After returning from that lamentable fiasco, he went back to my Ranch. In May, 1876, he joined the command of Col. Merritt as scout for the 5th U. S. Cavalry, attracted the special attention of General Crook and his officers, and gained their respect and confidence. He was at my Ranch at the time the Indians killed Jim Hunton and ran off all of my mules and horses.

"He married a daughter of M. A. Mouseau, made his home in camps in the Fort Fetterman neighborhood, and worked on wood and hay contracts for me until 1880. His last service at Fort Laramie was a courier between that place and Fort Robinson and

Bordeaux in 1890. I could write a great more concerning his life, all commendatory.

"He was called 'Little Bat' to distinguish him from Baptiste Pourier . . . One was 'Big Bat' and the other 'Little Bat'. General Crook considered Little Bat as one of his most valuable scouts and best hunter . . . "

The story of how Little Bat was murdered comes to light in a letter written many years ago by the late Capt. James Cook, of Agate, Nebraska, to his life-long friend, Russell Thorp, Jr. of Cheyenne. It happened something like this.

In 1898, Garnier was employed as post guide and interpreter at Fort Robinson, Nebraska, where he was a favorite among both officers and men. One day, about Christmas, 1900, Little Bat and an acquaintance entered a saloon in Crawford, Nebraska, for a glass of beer. The establishment was owned by a man named Dietrich, and the bartender was one Jim Haguewood, described by Capt. Cook as "having some family troubles and drinking quite heavily".

As Garnier and his friend were chatting over their beer, Haguewood is said to have angrily demanded, "Who pays for these drinks?" Little Bat replied, "I will when I am ready", and started unbuttoning his heavy buffalo hide coat to get his money from an inside pocket. Haguewood shouted, "You are ready right now" and grabbed a revolver. Garnier, himself unarmed, sensed that the man intended to shoot and crouched down in front of the bar. His assailant reached across it and fired, with the muzzle of his gun almost touching Little Bat's neck.

The fatally wounded man walked out of the saloon and toward his horse, but collapsed in the street. He was carried to a nearby room where he died in the arms of his wife some two hours later. She said afterward that before losing consciousness, he spoke to her in the Sioux language --- saying he thought

Haguewood was his friend and could not see why a friend should shoot him.

The killing was witnessed by several persons, but all of Little Bat's army friends were in Cuba when Haguewood stood trial for murder. He was acquitted because, in Capt. Cook's opinion, he was a white man while Little Bat, to most of the people in Crawford at least, was "nothing but an Indian". Capt. Cook also believed Baptiste Garnier's character and quarter-century of service to the army entitled him to a more fitting monument than the simple marker at his grave in Fort Robinson, with the single word "Employee" under his name and date of death.

But although the white side of half-breed Garnier's family tree may have treated his memory a big shabbily, some of his red brothers did not forget, according to this item in the *Crawford Gazette* of December 28, 1900.

> "There were several Indians on the Elkhorn train Tuesday morning enroute from Pine Ridge to Fort Robinson to attend the funeral of Baptiste Garnier. Some of the passengers were . . . a little alarmed when the redskins suddenly commenced to give vent to their lamentations with a weird and incomprehensible death chant. The timid ones were informed that there was no cause for alarm, after which they were deeply impressed with the novelty of the occasion. The chant was repeated several times."

Mon, July 10 [1876] --- (Nath) Williams, McMillan & others started with teams to Med. Bow. (Sam) Groves' & John Boyd teams with them . . .

The following episode [written for the *Fort Laramie Scout* by John Hunton] gives a better picture of John Boyd and some other individuals mentioned from time to time in his journal.

"In the winter of 1869 and 1870, Ben Mills, who had a small herd of stock cattle on the Laramie River and had suffered heavily from Indian depredations, moved the herd to Chugwater Creek, and in the early summer the herders, David Cottier, John Boyd, and William Aug, established their camp at the north mouth of Richard's Creek. They lived in a tent and had three horses with which they did all the herding and team work.

"One morning in April, 1870, Mr. Cottier took the team and wagon and went to Fort Laramie for supplies, leaving the one horse with Boyd and Aug. They had four milk cows and kept the calves confined in a small pen to entice the cows to come up at night. After Cottier left for the Fort, they (Boyd and Aug) milked the cows and turned them out of the pen. They then took their rifles and walked to the top of some hills nearby to see if the cattle were much scattered. They thought they were away from the camp about four hours or more.

"After getting back to camp, feeling very tired, they went into the tent and pulled off their boots to rest . . . and were lying down on their beds, which were buffalo robes spread on the ground, when a volley was fired by Indians through the tent. Each man grabbed his rifle and a cartridge belt and dashed out of the tent through the willows and into Chugwater Creek. As they had been lying flat on the ground, they were fortunately not touched by the bullets fired by the Indians. They were then in the Chugwater Creek barefooted and with no coats, four miles from Bordeaux and eight miles below Chugwater station. As the Indians saw them go into the willows with their rifles, they knew it would be dangerous to expose themselves.

"Boyd had been a soldier and had campaigned in Florida and Oregon against Indians, and had been twice wounded by arrows, so he was not easily excited. After deliberating a short time, he and Aug decided it would be safest to go up the creek, as the banks of the creek were much higher and there was more timber than there was downstream. They took time and great care. The Indians discovered them in the creek below Chimney Rock and fired several shots at them, and about a mile above Chimney Rock, they were shot at again but not hit. Boyd and Aug did not fire a shot.

"There was a camp of white men and half-breeds at the point of rocks two miles below Chugwater station, which Boyd and Aug reached before dark, and they were well cared for there. The next day, they and a party of men went to their camp and found the Indians had killed the four cows and four calves and burned the tent and everything connected with the camp."

Tues, Jan 9 [1877] --- Coach north.
Voorhees on Coach . . .

Luke Voorhees, reputed to have traveled the Oregon Trail in 1859, became one of the best-known names in early Wyoming stage coach history. He carried the first mail and express over the Cheyenne-Deadwood Black Hills Trail in 1876 and was one of the operators of the famed "Treasure Coach", which carried up to $300,000 in gold at a time, under heavy guard, from the Black Hills to Cheyenne. It therefore became a favorite target for road agents, [as illustrated in the previous section by the description of the Cold Springs stage robbery, based on Mr. Voorhees' account of that incident]. Voorhees also operated stage lines running from southern Wyoming into Colorado and engaged in mining. As Treasurer of Wyoming Territory, he was one of the first officials to occupy the new capitol building in Cheyenne.

> *Thurs, Mar 1 [1877] --- [Fort Laramie]*
> *Council of Administration met and recom-*
> *mended Mr. Bullock to be appointed Sutler.*

W. G. Bullock, Hunton's earliest partner in the cattle business, was the one person to whom he always gives the respectful title of "Mr.", even in his diary. Bullock was one of the few Hunton really "looked up to", and his high esteem for him continued throughout their long and close relationship. When Mr. Bullock died many years later, Hunton sadly recorded that he had lost the best and truest friend he ever had.

> *Sun, Mar 25 [1877] --- (John) Owens &*
> *family here. Loaned him plow.*

The Owens were Hunton's close neighbors, their ranch being four or five miles from Bordeaux on the road to the Black Hills. Johnny Owens had a rather remarkable career and unusual reputation as a professional gambler, sporting house proprietor (he, at one time, operated the Three Mile "Hog Ranch" just outside the Fort Laramie military reservation), and also as a highly-respected, honest citizen and "two-gun" sheriff with some 20 killings to his credit. Fine clothing and fine horses were said to be his hobbies.

Fri, April 27 [1877] --- Powell and I went to Post (Fetterman). Promised Capt. Pollock a cow . . .

Capt. Edwin Pollock was one of the officers assigned in 1875 to the impossible task of keeping miners out of the Black Hills, in accordance with the terms of our treaty with the Indians. And apparently he really tried. He had his troops arrest all the "invaders" they could catch and turned them over to the civil authorities. But it must have been frustrating work. The civil authorities just turned them loose to try and try again.

The good captain retired from his hazardous job of patrolling the wild frontier in 1885, only to almost immediately fall down the stairs of Cheyenne's Inter-Ocean Hotel and kill himself.

Wed, May 2 [1877] --- Bids opened for beef for (Forts) Reno and Fetterman. Lowest bid for Reno, J. R. Smith . . .

John R. Smith was an early rancher on Powder River who sold beef to the military and was reputed to be well-to-do. One day a notorious road agent, one Frank Towle, came to Smith's ranch bent on robbery. Instead, Smith shot Towle. And then Mrs. Smith nursed the bandit back to health. For this broadminded if not loving care, the gallant Towle is understood to have shown his appreciation, later on, by stealing Smith's horses. After all, business is business.

Fri, May 18 [1877] --- Billy Bacon went to lower roundup for Phillips . . .

Whatever their failings and shortcomings may have been, Billy Bacon and one Jack Sanders carved a permanent niche for themselves in Wyoming history a few years after the above entry. About December 1, 1885, they quarreled, met with blazing guns, and blasted each other into eternity.

On May 4, 1950 the late C. W. (Charlie) Horr wrote his recollections of that doubly-fatal duel in a letter to Wyoming State Engineer L. C. Bishop, as follows.

> "Bacon came to LaBonte in about 1879 and ran a road ranch at the crossing . . . Sold his (squatter's) right to Harry Pollard's father in the spring of 1883 for $5,000. Then he went to Cheyenne and was drinking and gambling, but some of his friends got him to leave, so he went back to LaBonte and bought a bunch of cows. He took the cows up to Bacon Park in June, '84. I saw him there. He had built a cabin and his wife was there in '85 or '86. He traded the cattle to Frank Gore --- 100 head --- for Frank's saloon in Fetterman, so that is how he came to be in Fetterman, and Sanders owned the dance hall.
>
> "Well, they fell out and started out to get each other. Bacon had a double-barreled shotgun and Sanders had a .45 six-shooter. When they met, Bacon shot Sanders in the stomach and Sanders shot Bacon in the throat. Sanders was badly shot and died . . . "

The late George H. Cross, pioneer rancher in the Fetterman area, gave his daughter, Mrs. Criss Cross Morton, a version of what happened to Bacon after the gunfight. Mrs. Morton wrote [to my grandfather] that the Fetterman physician, Dr. Amos Barber, was on the road from Fetterman to Rock Creek when the shooting occurred, and a man was sent on horseback to try to overtake and bring him back. Meanwhile, when Sanders died, they loaded the wounded Bacon in a buckboard and started out with a fast team, hoping to meet the doctor. But by the time they reached Buckshot, Billy was bleeding so badly and suffering so much that they stopped there, and Sam Slaymaker and others used a spoon to try to remove the bullet, which slipped down the hapless gunman's windpipe and choked him to death. After that, folks around Buckshot all talked about Billy Bacon's ghost haunting the place.

Fri, July 26 [1878] --- Hay camp last night. Went back, met bull outfit. Cary's (Carey's) herd arrived . . .

[By the time the above entry was made], John Hunton had gradually moved his beef herd from Bordeaux to his ranch on Box Elder Creek near Fort Fetterman, his principal market. This location later became the celebrated Careyhurst Ranch, established by Joseph M. Carey and his brothers, who also acquired Hunton's "SO" brand. The arrival of "Cary's herd" along the Box Elder on that July day may have been the start of it all.

In addition to establishing one of the best-known ranches and cattle herds in the west, Joseph M. Carey carved a remarkable political career for himself in this new land. After serving as Territorial U. S. Attorney, he was appointed a justice of the Territorial Supreme Court by President Grant in 1871. Judge Carey served three terms as mayor of Cheyenne, where he owned and developed considerable downtown business property. In 1884, he was elected Territorial Delegate to the 49th Congress and twice returned to that office. He is credited with introducing the legislation which made Wyoming a state. And the new state sent him back to Washington as Wyoming's first United States Senator in 1890. In 1911, he was elected governor. His sons, Robert and Charles, followed in their father's political footsteps, with Robert's career leading to the governorship in 1919 and later to the United States Senate. Thus did the Careys become and remain one of Wyoming's most illustrious families for two generations.

Thurs, May 1 [1879] --- Thorp & Dave
passed to Deadwood with horses...

The name "Thorp" has been closely woven into Wyoming history for more than three-quarters of a century. Russell Thorp was one of the founders and operators of the first stage line from Cheyenne to the Black Hills. He was a dealer in fine horses and mules, which he sold and trailed not only north through hostile Indian country into the Black Hills of the Dakota Territory, but also as far south as Leadville, Colorado.

He mined and sold coal to the Union Pacific Railroad in the 1860's, and operated a store and livery stable in southwestern Wyoming where, at the age of twenty-three, he was appointed to the first board of commissioners of Uinta county by Territorial Governor John D. Campbell.

In 1882, Mr. Thorp purchased the Adkins ranch in Raw Hide Buttes, complete with a blacksmith shop, general store, stage coach stop with ample road ranch accommodations for travelers, post office, and telegraph service. It continued to be his home and headquarters for many years. He was killed in a runaway at Lusk, Wyoming on September 8, 1898, at the age of fifty-two.

His son, Russell Thorp, Jr., carried on where the father left off. He could, and did, drive a four-horse stage coach at the age of fourteen. In later life, he was secretary of the Wyoming Stock Growers Association for many years. Perhaps no other one man has ever done more to preserve the traditions and history of Wyoming pioneer days than Russell Thorp, Jr., [as illustrated by the quantity of information and photographs provided by Mr. Thorp to my grandfather for inclusion in his books about John Hunton's diaries].

Fri, May 2 [1879] --- Mr. Frewen here
last night going to Powder River . . .

Moreton and Dick Frewen were British sportsmen of considerable means who came to Wyoming on a hunting trip in 1876 and remained to organize the Powder River Cattle Company. On that fabled stream, they built a luxurious establishment that was known far and wide during the high-flying 1880's as "Frewen's Castle". And there these gentlemen lavishly entertained the elite of Wyoming society as well as lords and ladies from overseas for weeks on end. But they, too, went broke in the great crash of 1887 and returned to England. The story is told that during those fulsome days, Moreton Frewen once shot a buffalo from his front steps. Some twenty years later, a friend wrote that his castle was gone --- but the skull of that buffalo was still there.

[John Hunton's accounting records for
August, 1879] --- [Paid] F. E. Warren $170.

Occasionally one meets interesting people in Mr. Hunton's "cash account". The F. E. Warren, for instance, to whom he paid $170 was destined to become the most influential man in the Congress of the United States in later years. He was the senior member of the U. S. Senate and chairman of its all-powerful appropriations committee when death ended his service. During the 1870's, Mr. Warren was known as the "merchant prince" of Cheyenne, and the firm with which he was associated, Converse

& Warren, did a large business selling "complete outfits" to miners headed for the Black Hills. Today's great air base at Cheyenne bears his name . . .

> *[John Hunton's accounting records for*
> *October, 1880] --- [Paid] Gen. Dodge $43.*

The "Gen. Dodge" to whom Mr. Hunton paid $43 was Gen. Grenville M. Dodge, the engineer who built the Union Pacific Railroad. After looking over the lay of the land, Gen. Dodge located the division point on Crow Creek and called it Cheyenne. Simultaneously, in accordance with instructions, Gen. C. C. Auger established a new military post adjoining the division point. It became Fort D. A. Russell, now the Warren air base. Gen. John A. Rawlins made a patriotic speech at the new post, which is said to have so impressed Gen. Dodge that he named another new town site on the route of the U. P. after the orator --- which is how Rawlins, Wyoming got its name.

While they were setting up Fort Russell, or Camp Carlin as it was originally known, Indians came swooping down Crow Creek and attacked a Mormon grading outfit coming in from Salt Lake to work on the railroad. Two men of the party were killed before soldiers came galloping to the rescue. Those two unfortunates were the first to be buried in Cheyenne's brand new cemetery.

The rails reached Cheyenne on November 13, 1867, and within a few months, the little frontier tent settlement and construction camp mushroomed into a city of some three thousand dwellings and business establishments. In September of that year, N. A. Baker came from Colorado to start the *Cheyenne Leader*, pioneer newspaper of the area. Thus Wyoming's capital city was born, and Gen. Dodge seems to have well-played the part assigned him in that page of history --- which is all any man can do in his brief mortal span.

Sat, Nov 6 [1880] --- Stimpson &
Hibbard here [at Bordeaux] tonight going
to Deadwood . . .

The "Hibbard" mentioned above was W. H. Hibbard, who
built the first telegraph line from Cheyenne to the Black Hills
during the summer of 1876, and was manager of the Cheyenne
and Black Hills Telegraph Company. To help finance construction of the line, Mr. Hibbard sold "scrip" to businessmen and
citizens in both Cheyenne and the "Hills", which the company
accepted in payment for telegraph service when the line was
completed.

It was a hazardous job. The country was swarming with
Indians who were mad as hornets at the white man's invasion of
their treasured hunting grounds. But the poles went up, and the
wires were strung. By September, you could send a telegram
from Hat Creek stage station to Cheyenne, and the line was
completed to Custer City on October 19th. But no telegrams
were actually sent from that gold rush capital until several weeks
later, as the Indians were almost as busy tearing down stretches
of the new line as the white men were building and repairing it
--- and service remained intermittent and uncertain until the
tribesmen were confined to reservations.

Thurs, Nov 3 [1881] --- Gen. Crook &
Mr. J. S. Collins called on us . . .

The J. S. Collins who, with Gen. [George] Crook, called on
John Hunton and his bride, had been post trader at Fort Laramie
from 1872 to 1877. Mr. Collins also built the Rustic Hotel at the
old Fort in 1876, and it became headquarters for the Cheyenne
and Black Hills Stage Company.

Fri, Oct 13 [1882] --- Dick Elgin killed
at Fetterman yesterday. Murderer hung . . .

In 1882, Fort Fetterman was abandoned as a military post. It was no longer needed. The Indians had been subdued. But the old fort, forerunner of the town of Douglas, remained as a settlement, trading center, and rendezvous for cattle men, cowboys, roundups, gamblers, dance hall girls, and kindred characters. It was in this tough and lawless place that Malcolm Campbell, then a young deputy, received experience which undoubtedly helped him become one of the most renowned sheriffs on the western frontier.

Here is a summary of Campbell's story of what happened that October night of 1882. Searight's roundup had come to town. It was gathering and tallying cattle which had been sold to the "CY" outfit. Altmen & Webel's saloon was crowded. In the milling, drinking crowd were two men quite different in character, but with one thing in common --- both were marked for violent death that night.

Dick Elgin, described by Campbell as a fine, upstanding man, was bookkeeper and paymaster for the Goose Egg ranch. He was chatting and swapping yarns with a small group of friends. At the bar, drinking heavily, was a Goose Egg cowboy, "Red" Capp, remembered by Campbell as "a big, red-headed, happy boy --- but whisky always made him half crazy".

Elgin had started to tell a story when Red swayed over to the group, grabbed Elgin by the arm, and spun him around, demanding money. The still-smiling Elgin told the drink-crazed cowboy that he had already overdrawn his wages, that he could not give him more money without authorization from Mr. Searight, suggested he'd better roll in --- and turned back to finish his story. Again Red spun Elgin around, said he would kill him if he did not fork over, gave the bookkeeper a violent shove, and jumped backward, hand on his still-holstered gun. In doing so, Capp stumbled and his triggerless weapon discharged, creasing his hip. Apparently thinking Elgin had fired on him, Red then drew and shot his victim through the mouth, into the brain. He then tried to escape on Elgin's own horse, which was tied outside, but the animal, appropriately enough, bucked off its master's murderer before they reached the nearby Platte River.

Malcolm Campbell was not present when the shooting occurred. He had been over to George Powell's ranch. But his brother Dan and a man named Moore captured the unseated killer near the Platte bridge, floundering around on foot. Malcolm came driving in as they returned with their prisoner, helped lock him up in the old army guardhouse, left Tom Walker on guard, and went home for his supper. Before Campbell finished his meal, Walker came to tell him that he needn't hurry --- the guard had been "surprised" and overpowered by a mob of Elgin's friends, and Red Capp was hanging from a log which jutted out from a corner of the jail.

Justice of the Peace John O'Brien held an inquest, the verdict being that Capp "came to his death by parties unknown to the jury". Then the cowboys, their obvious duty done, all turned to and gave Red a big and proper funeral.

Fri, Apr 13 [1883] --- Deep snow on ground. Gov. Hoyt here [at Bordeaux]...

John W. Hoyt was appointed governor of Wyoming Territory in 1878 and almost immediately launched a vigorous campaign against the gangs of road agents and stage robbers who preyed upon the travelers and commerce of that day. He is also credited with being one of the first to push for establishment of an institution of higher education in the territory, and during his first year in office reported to the Secretary of the Interior that plans for a college were underway. However, actual authorization to build a university in the City of Laramie was not passed by the territorial legislature until 1886. As was natural, a spirited contest developed in that legislature over where the capitol and the university would be located. Editorial comment of the day indicates that when Cheyenne got the capitol and Laramie the university, both communities were fairly well satisfied.

Tues, July 3 [1883] --- John Thomas,
Guernsey and Arbuckle here [at Bordeaux]
tonight . . .

Charles A. Guernsey came to Wyoming Territory from Albany, New York in 1880, settling on the Cheyenne River. He was primarily a mining man and, in 1889, secured copper and iron claims along the North Platte River some fifteen or twenty miles above Fort Laramie, where the large Colorado Fuel & Iron Co. mines later located. Mr. Guernsey also started the town which bears his name and founded one of the best-known stock ranches on the Platte River. He served in the Wyoming Territorial legislature and later in the state senate, of which body he became president. Another monument to his name and activity is the Guernsey dam, reservoir, and power plant on the Platte. He is said to have advocated the dam's construction forty years before it was actually built.

Sat, Mar 29 [1884] --- Number of men
. . . at Ranch, including Tisdale, Weston,
Reeder, deHemecourt & others . . .

The "Tisdale" who stayed over at Bordeaux was probably John A. Tisdale, who lived in Johnson County some 60 miles from Buffalo, Wyoming. On November 30, 1891, Mr. Tisdale started to Buffalo with his team and wagon for winter supplies. That was a time of strife and violence on the range. Before reaching his destination, Tisdale heard that his life had been threatened by a stockman and former sheriff named Frank M. Canton, and he bought a double-barreled shotgun for protection on his way home.

About seven miles out of Buffalo, and some three miles beyond the Cross H ranch, Tisdale was shot to death from a gulch near the road. His team and heavily-loaded wagon, with the dead man still on it, were then driven beyond sight of the road where the horses were also shot to death. Mr. Canton was arrested and charged with the murder but was released after a hearing before Justice of the Peace Parmalee.

This was but one of several killings leading to the "Johnson County War", about which a number of books have been written. David's "Malcolm Campbell, Sheriff" presents the case for the cattlemen "invaders". Mercer's "Banditti of the Plains" champions the small settlers, the so-called "rustlers". Neither book makes much pretense at impartial or objective reporting. Passion and prejudice ran too high for that in those good old days.

Tues, June 3 [1884] --- Dined with
Harry Yount [at Bordeaux] . . .

Harry S. Yount, with whom John Hunton dined on June 3, 1884, was a rather remarkable fellow --- a combination soldier, frontiersman, scout, explorer, mountain climber, miner, trapper, and hunter. He was born in Susquehanna County, Pennsylvania on March 18, 1847, enlisted in the Union army at the age of 14, served throughout the Civil War, and came to Wyoming as a bull freighter in 1866.

In 1873, Mr. Yount joined Dr. Hayden's Geological Survey, with which he spent a number of years exploring the then-

uncharted mountain country of Wyoming. During 1878, he and
a mountain-climbing Professor A. D. Wilson of this survey scaled
the Grand Tetons. President Hayes, in 1880, appointed Harry
Yount "gamekeeper" of Yellowstone Park, and Younts Peak, at
the head of the Yellowstone River, was named after him.

But apparently that life was too tame and in 1882, he started
his own hunting and trapping career, ranging over much of the
west and all of the game country in what is now Wyoming,
stopping now and then to do a little prospecting. He ended up
with considerable mining property, including a marble stone
quarry.

There are a number of stories and fables about Harry Yount's
prowess as a hunter of big game, but he was probably best-known
as a bear killer and is reputed to have, on occasion, followed the
beasts right into their dens for showdown, hand-to-paw combat,
where it was a case of win --- or else. He was also friend and
companion of another noted bear hunter, "Dutch" George Ware,
who was killed by a grizzly, exact date unknown, in the Laramie
Peak region. Ware's body, skull crushed and one leg chewed up,
was found and buried by Johnny Gordon.

> *Mon, July 23 [1888] --- Come here [to*
> *Cheyenne] today on county business . . .*
> *John Clay on train.*

Few men have left a deeper imprint on early Wyoming
history than John Clay, Scotch money lender, cattle raiser,
writer, historian, and businessman. After graduation from the
University of Edinburgh, he came to America in 1874 and to
Wyoming about 1882, where he made many large loans of British
and European capital to cattle outfits. In later years, he organized
Clay, Robinson & Co., which eventually became the John Clay
Livestock Commission Co., one of the nation's largest.

Some historians credit John Clay with helping Maj. Frank Wolcott (who is said to have owed Clay $80,000) plan the Johnson County invasion of 1892. But this Mr. Clay denied, saying that when Wolcott told him in 1891 of the plan he had in mind, he strongly advised the doughty major against it. And Clay was in Europe the following year when the abortive "invasion" was actually undertaken. He said he did not even know about it until he read the story in an Irish newspaper, and later wrote that it probably would not have happened at all had he been in Wyoming. But he did play a leading part in getting the "invaders" off scot-free after their surrender and phony imprisonment.

After the failure of the Swan Brothers, [as documented in "The Rise and Fall of Fortune" section of chapter 1], who were also said to have been heavily financed with Clay capital, he took over the management of that outfit for a while. In fact, through the foreign capital which he represented, a great many, if not most, of the early "cattle barons" were deeply in debt to John Clay, and he thus exercised considerable power and influence over them --- the power of financial life or death, in some cases.

A Few More Names and Faces
From Wyoming's Pioneer Era

[The following paraphrased excerpts from Pat Flannery's narratives in his fascinating books alphabetically profile a handful more of the noteworthy Wyoming pioneers mentioned by John Hunton in his diary entries.]

H. E. BROWN

"Stuttering" Brown came to Cheyenne from Salt Lake City in 1876 as the business agent for Gilmer, Salisbury, and Patrick, leading stage coach operators of that day. He was later made superintendent of the first stage line from Fort Laramie to the Black Hills. Brown was fatally wounded on a trail north of Hat Creek Station either by Indians or by stage robber Persimmon Bill Chambers (apparently no one ever knew for sure).

BILLY BULLOCK
Photo Courtesy of
Agnes Wright Spring

Billy was the half-breed son of W. G. Bullock (Mr. Hunton's best and truest friend), who worked for Hunton off and on for a number of years. He later became a rider with the famous "Buffalo Bill" Cody Wild West Show.

MALCOMB CAMPBELL
Photo Courtesy of
Warren Richardson

Campbell was John Hunton's friend and business associate in the 1870's and later became one of the Old West's most famous lawmen. In the photo shown above, the boarded-up opening behind Campbell is a window of the room shared by Hunton and scout Jim Bridger during the winter of 1867.

"FRENCHY" CAZABON

Frenchy was a little peddler who roamed the frontier with his store on wheels. He was very popular, especially with the children, for whom he always had candy. Cazabon trusted everyone, and sold even the passing cowboys anything he had on credit --- and seldom lost a bill.

CHARLES E. CLAY
Photo Courtesy of
Clement Ayers

Mr. Clay, born in Virginia in 1839, served in the Confederate army and came West after the Civil War. He and Hunton developed two of the biggest ox-team freight hauling outfits in the territory. Charles was later a member of Wyoming's first State Legislature, the first Douglas town council, and a local judge. While serving as marshal of Elma, Washington in 1905, the 67-year-old Clay received fatal injuries while trying to arrest an obstreperous drunk.

WILLIAM M. DAILEY
Photo Courtesy of
Mrs. C. C. Morton

Nicknamed "Long" because he was well over six feet tall, Mr. Dailey was born in Ohio in 1836 and raised on an Indiana farm. He and his brother, John L. Dailey, came to Colorado in 1859, had a try at mining, and then went to Denver, where William put up the building in which his brother and William N. Byers published *The Rocky Mountain News*. William raised cattle in Colorado during the 1860's and 1870's. In 1875, Dailey and others drove their Colorado herds to LaBonte Creek near Fort Fetterman, probably the first beef cattle in that area of Wyoming. In 1877, he sold his ranch, returned to Colorado, married, and took up a homestead.

GEORGE FERRIS

Mr. Ferris, a Union soldier, came to Wyoming a year or two after the Civil War, went into the cattle business, and later into mining. In 1902, the Ferris-Haggerty mine in Carbon County, of which he was then said to be the sole owner, was sold to the North American Copper Mining Company for $1,000,000.

H. GLAFCKE

Editor of the *Cheyenne Leader* and also mayor of the Magic City in those rip-snorting days, Glafcke fought mightily with his pen and influence to keep Cheyenne (instead of Sidney and Omaha, Nebraska) as the outfitting center for the Black Hills. In 1876, Mr. Glafcke, F. E. Warren, and M. E. Post successfully persuaded the Post Office Department to change the mail routing for Deadwood and "The Hills" from Sidney to Cheyenne. Had it not been for the determined efforts of such men, Wyoming's development and future railroad construction might have taken a different course.

GEORGE HARRIS

Mr. Harris was one of the few survivors of the "Bloody Trail Massacre" of original settlers on Horseshoe Creek, northwest of Fort Laramie, in 1868. Harris lay wounded in the brush all night watching the settlement burn, and finally reached safety somehow.

W. C. IRVINE

"Billy" Irvine came to Wyoming from Pennsylvania in the 1870's and associated with large cattle interests. He was active in both the Wyoming Stock Growers and American National Cattle Growers Associations. Irvine was one of the leaders in the Johnson County Invasion; a man of determination, fearless and relentless in fighting cattle "rustlers". He also later served as a Wyoming state senator and treasurer.

ANTOINE JANIS

Antoine, the brother of Nick Janis, was a rancher as well as a stage station operator with whom John Hunton did much hay business. Some authorities say that his Indian wife was a daughter of Sioux Chief Red Cloud. In 1872 on Christmas Day, Antoine's half-breed sons William and Pete were killed by Joseph and James Richard in a tragic brawl.

CHARLES KING

Mr. King served in the 1876 campaign against the Sioux and was appointed adjutant of his regiment by Gen. Merritt. He was forced to temporarily retire from active military duty in 1879, with the rank of captain, because of an old wound received in a fight with Apache Indians at Sunset Pass in 1874. In 1898, recovered in health, King volunteered for the War with Spain and was appointed as Brigadier General of Volunteers. He wrote many novels

(Continued on the next page)

CHARLES KING
(continued)

of military life, which included "Campaigning With Crook" and perhaps the most famous of all, "Laramie or the Queen of Bedlam" --- exciting tales of the mysterious goings-on in Old Bedlam, the bachelor officers' quarters at Ft. Laramie.

THE OELRICH BROTHERS

C. M. and Harry Oelrich were among those dashing, wealthy young men who came west to get in on the fabulous and get-rich-quick cattle boom of the 1800's. C. M. was one of the original incorporators of the Cheyenne Club, while Harry became famous for the parties he threw at his place on Crow Creek. Harry's English drag, imported at a reputed cost of over $4000, must have been the equivalent of today's expensive, custom-built limos. English actress Lily Langtry was one of the many cuties he used to take riding in it, 'tis said.

SAMUEL SLAYMAKER
Photo Courtesy of
Douglas Budget

A quartermaster sergeant at Fort Fetterman, Slaymaker was said to have been known affectionately as "Slippery" due to his alleged cooperation in slipping local civilians a bit of useful army material now and then --- such as a keg of nails, when needed. In later life, he served as justice of the peace, clerk of the Converse County district court and also its first assessor, and was receiver of the Douglas U. S. Land Office.

FRED ST. DENNIS

Fred St. Dennis and George H. Cross were schoolmates in Montreal and came to Colorado together in 1874. Mr. Cross leaves the record that St. Dennis was a well-educated young man of French-Scottish ancestry. He married a school teacher, Edna Holland. After he established his road ranch on Horseshoe Creek in 1879, St. Dennis began drinking to excess, finally lost all he had at the Cheyenne gambling tables --- and shot himself.

SPEED STAGNER

Mr. Stagner apparently left his home in Missouri during the early 1860's and cut all family ties. He was a trusted scout for General George Crook on the March, 1876 expedition against the Sioux. According to Mrs. Criss Cross Morton, Speed was Little Bat Garnier's brother-in-law. One of his wives was half-breed (probably Lallee's sister), and the other two were Sioux and Shoshone. Their offspring were numerous.

MRS. JOHN R. STEELE (NANNIE CLAY)

Nannie Clay and her brother, Charles, were second cousins of the statesman Henry Clay. They came from Virginia to Wyoming Territory in 1876. John R. Steele, a young Englishman who worked for the Swan Land and Cattle Company, married her on January 26, 1881. When she was a little girl in Virginia, Nannie witnessed the surrender of General Robert E. Lee at Appomattox from a perch in the uppermost branches of a cherry tree.

WILLIAM SWAN

William was one of the four fabulous Swans of Scottish descent who were destined to build Wyoming's greatest cattle dynasty. They began operations about 1873, and by 1887, more than 100,000 head of Swan cattle were grazing on the overcrowded range. The company's book assets totaled in the neighborhood of three million dollars when the great blizzards of 1886-87 came --- resulting in the Swan clan, banks, business houses, and lesser cattlemen, including John Hunton, going broke, as recounted in chapter 1. It was the end of an era.

ELIAS W. WHITCOMB

Whitcomb was John Hunton's neighbor and one of the best-known Wyoming pioneers. He settled on Horseshoe Creek about 1861 and, at one time, ran a trading store which was burned down by a gang of outlaws. Whitcomb was later one of the famous "Johnson County Invaders". His Indian wife was related to Baptiste (Little Bat) and Lallee Garnier.

CHAPTER 4

GLIMPSES OF THINGS TO COME

[You probably have noticed that many incidents recorded in John Hunton's diaries had minimal, if any, direct impact on his life, but that some of these were linked by the writings of Mr. Hunton, Pat Flannery, and others to events which ultimately would prove to be rather significant in the annals of Wyoming history, and in some cases, to our entire nation. A few more examples of such diary entries and related passages are presented in this chapter.]

Tues, Jan 29 [1878] --- Bond election
[for a railroad subsidy]. Squaws voted . . .

An intriguing feature of this 1878 polling, to us at least, is that Mr. Hunton again took pains to record, as he did in previous elections, that the "Squaws voted" right along with their white men. Wyoming takes proper pride in having been the first state to give women the right to vote. But whatever additional and progressive motives may have inspired Wyoming's founding fathers to thus extend the franchise to their women, it appears clear that they were also maintaining a precedent and tradition established by the original pioneers of earliest territorial days when most of their wives or female companions were native daughters of the Sioux.

Mon, July 29 [1878] --- Went to Cotton-
wood. Witnessed total eclipse of the sun
between LaBontee and Horse Shoe . . .

That total eclipse of the sun is said to have created a lot of interest throughout the Territory of Wyoming --- more interest, at any rate, than did the party of early scientists who came from the east to make observations of the event from atop the continental divide in south-central Wyoming. And apparently only the slightest ripple of interest was aroused by a certain unobtrusive little chap who was a member of that expedition --- Thomas A. Edison by name.

The story goes that on this trip, young Edison, while fishing on the shore of Battle Lake, near the present town of Encampment, fell to contemplating a few bamboo threads he had pulled off his fishing pole. They gave him an idea which kicked around in his remarkable brain until it led eventually to the development of a filament which enabled him to make the first incandescent electric lamp. Odd how important little things sometimes turn out to be. All the excitement about that long-forgotten eclipse --- just a flash in the pan of passing events. But the young fellow idly fishing and thinking beside a Wyoming mountain lake had a flash in his head which literally turned night into day for all the civilized world.

Fri, Sept 6 [1878] --- Started to (Fort) Fetterman. Nooned at Gordon's . . .

Early in the spring of 1878, a young man from Ireland, but of Scotch ancestry, and with quite a flair for poetry, came out of Colorado looking for a new home in Wyoming. His name was Johnny Gordon. On a previous visit, he had stayed with John Hunton at Bordeaux, took a fancy to the country between the North and South Laramie Rivers, and decided to settle there, near Uva.

He built and operated a road ranch and became a one-man chamber of commerce for irrigation. Among his patrons was

Joseph M. Carey, [who was profiled in the previous chapter], and Gordon "sold" his influential guest on the possibilities for irrigating the area. The Wheatland irrigation project eventually resulted, and Carey, in later years, heralded Johnny Gordon as the father of that development. [This pioneering effort and subsequent irrigation projects significantly helped Wyoming's agricultural production to flourish, thus generating sales in the billions of dollars.]

[Our final glimpse of the future in this chapter comes not from Mr. Hunton's diaries, but rather from the following manuscript, written on pencil tablet paper in his hand, which my grandfather came upon while thumbing through a box of John Hunton's letters and papers.]

"In 1873 or 1874, I was hauling freight for the U. S. from Medicine Bow Station on the [Union Pacific Railroad] to Fort Fetterman. In late summer or early fall of the year, Michell Lajuenesse, a half-breed Indian, told me and others that while on a hunt north of Casper, he saw a place on the ground where there was oil on top of the dirt and that he scraped some of it up and cleaned it by warming and used it to grease his wagon.

"The subject was occasionally spoken of until finally he, Baptiste Garnier, and myself rigged up an outfit and went on the hunt for that place. We went from Fetterman to Fort Casper and crossed the Platte River just below where the bridge stood and went northward about 25 or 30 miles . . . About night the day of leaving Casper, we came to a little stream and went into camp.

"Next morning, Mr. Lajuenesse showed 'Bat' and I where he had scraped up the oil . . . [at or near

'Teapot Rock']. We went to work, and each one scraped up a small quantity of the stuff when about 25 or 30 Arapahoe Indians suddenly came upon us, but in a friendly way.

"They held a few minutes conversation with Lajuenesse, who understood their language, and disappeared as suddenly as they had appeared. Lajuenesse told me the Indians had ordered us away and for us not to come back. We immediately started and did not stop until we had crossed to the south side of the Platte River.

"The three of us had gathered a quart bottle more than half full of the stuff after most of the dirt and gravel had been separated from it . . . I took the bottle of oil to Medicine Bow Station and left it with Mr. Wm. H. Taylor to be examined to ascertain if it was valuable. Lajuenesse and I paid no further attention to it, and so the matter dropped.

"[A number of years later], I met Mr. Taylor in Cheyenne and in reminiscing over old times, this 'bottle' came up. He told me that when he was packing up the office fixtures at Medicine Bow Station in 1876 to move them to Rockcreek Station, he found this bottle of oil among the old rubbish he was moving and took it to Rockcreek, but did not take further care of it and could not tell what finally became of it."

Mr. Hunton's adventure apparently took place in an area destined to later become one of the world's largest light oil producing fields --- and a household word during the great Teapot Dome scandal of the Harding administration in the early 1920's. [To summarize the details of this notorious episode in American history, these petroleum reserves and others in California were set aside by the federal government in case they would later be needed by the U. S. Navy. They were put under the control of Albert Fall, Secretary of the Interior, who then secretly leased some of the fields to several big oil companies in return for a few hundred thousand dollars in "gifts". When the scheme was uncovered, Albert truly became the "Fall" guy for this affair, being levied a large fine and sentenced to jail time, while the oilmen involved got what amounted to a slap on the wrist. Government watchdogs became more vigilant after that in trying to detect political and business corruption, but as we know from current events, they haven't stopped some individuals from trying to follow in Mr. Fall's footprints.]

[In retrospect, it seems a bit of a shame that John Hunton didn't continue trying to determine if the "stuff" he and his party discovered was of any value. If he had, we might have been able to add "oil magnate" to Mr. Hunton's list of careers.]

EPILOGUE

BULL WHACKING ON RUBBER TIRES
- A JOURNEY TO RECAPTURE THE PAST -

This is the summary of a trip over dim and long-deserted trails from Cheyenne, Wyoming, north to the sites of ancient forts and stage stations that were once havens of safety for weary travelers and the rendezvous of pioneers --- to places now almost lost to sight and memory.

Wyoming's energetic State Engineer L. C. Bishop had a passion for new information on old trails and almost forgotten historic sites which puts to shame a smoker's yearning for his cigarette or a drinker's thirst for his bottle. In mid-January, 1956, this urge sent Mr. Bishop bounding over the Wyoming winter landscape along bull-train and stage coach routes of the state's pioneer era. Snow and howling January winds added a touch of realism over much of the way. Albert Sims and Lyle Hildebrand, of Douglas, went along to open the barbed-wire gates, of which there were probably not more than a thousand in all. [Pat Flannery] also went along.

[Maps which include the historic trails and sites visited by these four latter-day explorers are presented on the following two pages and were prepared by Mr. Bishop specifically for inclusion in my grandfather's books. They are shown here for your reference as you continue reading about the travelers' journey over the Wyoming range and into frontier times, at least in their mind's eye.]

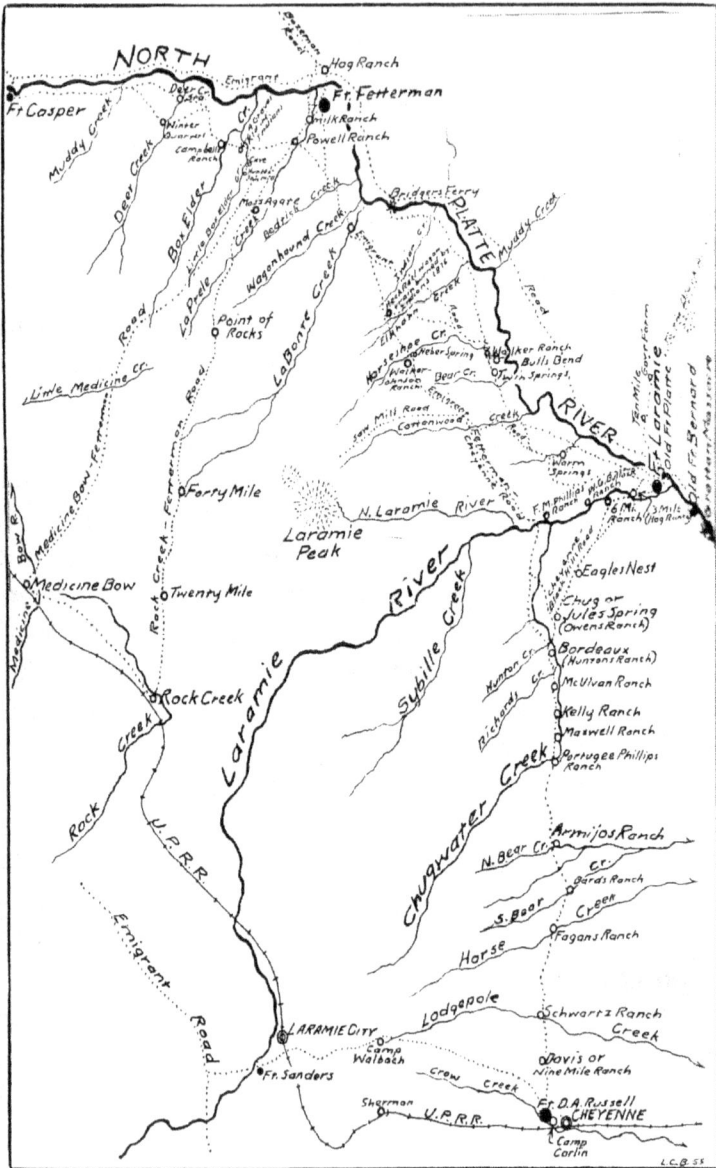

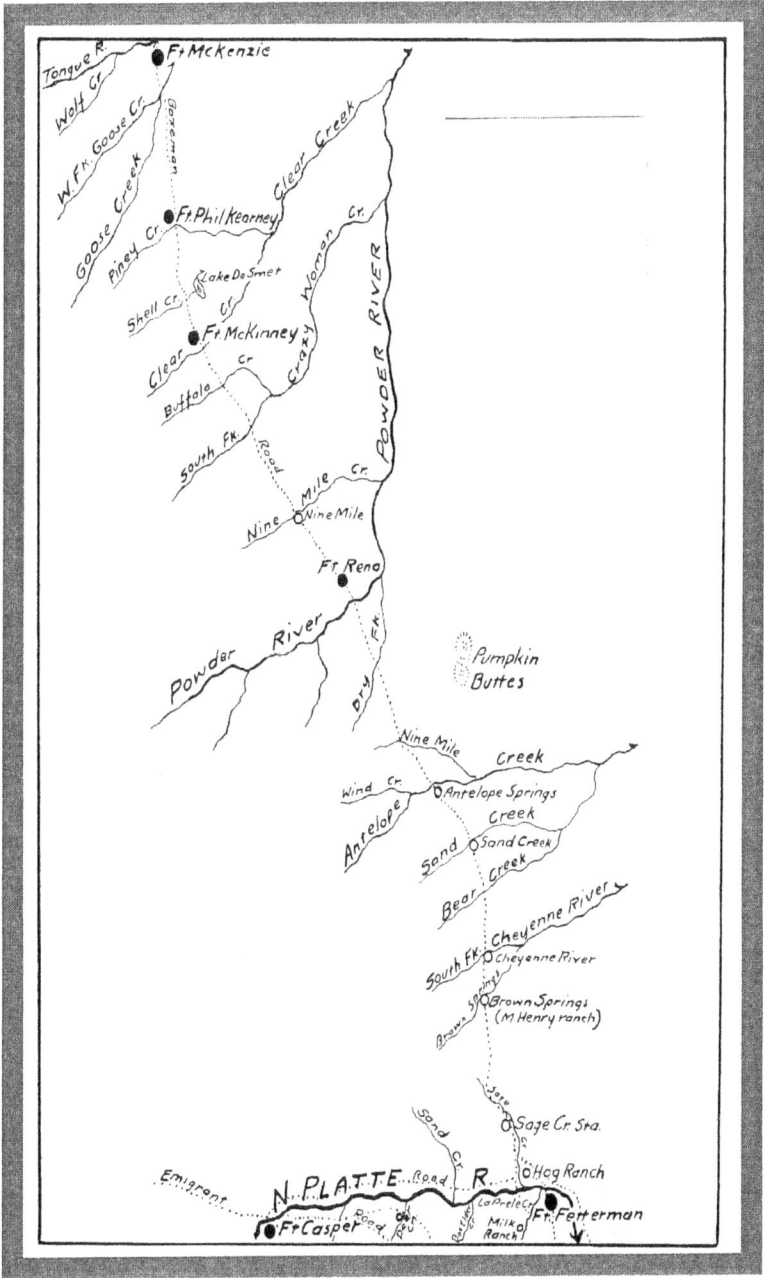

Tongue R.

Wolf Cr.

Ft. McKenzie

W. Fk. Goose Cr.

Goose Creek

Bozeman

Clear Creek

Ft. Phil Kearney

Piney Cr.

Cr.

Woman

Lake De Smet

Shell Cr.

Cr.

Clear

Ft. McKinney

Buffalo

Cr.

Crazy

South Fk.

Road

POWDER RIVER

Nine Mile Cr.

Nine Mile

Nine Mile

Ft. Reno

Powder River

Dry Fk.

Pumpkin Buttes

Nine Mile Creek

Wind Cr.

Antelope Springs

Antelope

Creek

Sand

Sand Creek

Bear Creek

South Fk.

Cheyenne River

Cheyenne River

Brown Springs

Brown Springs
(M Henry ranch)

Jere

Sage Cr. Sta.

Sand Cr.

Hog Ranch

Emigrant

Road

N. PLATTE R.

Road

Road

Ft. Casper

La Prele Cr.

Box Elder

Milk Ranch

Ft. Fetterman

The trip started from old Camp Carlin, which was located between Cheyenne and the adjacent Warren Air Base. From there the dim trail leads north across gently rolling prairie to the old Davis, or Nine Mile, Ranch. Mr. Adamson, whose home is in that area, directed us to the site of the old well and cellar dugouts, which are about all that remain of that first stop on the long and lonely trail. A certain "Madame" Selig later took over and built a sporting house at Nine Mile Ranch, which became a popular resort for soldiers, freighters, and other local gentry. Nothing resembling that kind of sport is around there today.

Another seven miles or so, always pushing northward except for detours around steep hills and badlands, brings you to Lodgepole Creek, where the Fred Schwartz road ranch and stage station once offered hospitality to man and beast. Its buildings have vanished, but there along the creek are the willows and brush to which Mrs. Schwartz, heavy with child, fled for refuge with her three-year-old daughter Minna when drink-crazed cowboys wrecked the place and broke into the family living quarters searching for "women". Mrs. Schwartz lost her unborn baby that brutal night, but little Minna lived and grew to become a beautiful chorus girl in the original "Prince of Pilsen" cast and later married the famous newspaper columnist, Franklin P. Adams.

By this time, if the unfamiliar traveler is not geographically confused by Wyoming's wide-open spaces, he should be. But what Clark Bishop calls his "hillbilly instinct" and unerring eagle eye for grass-covered ruts of the old trail carry you on north another eight or ten miles to Horse Creek and the Nimmo ranch of today. There, in a thicket-like cluster of trees near the modern house, stands a beautifully-weathered, long-abandoned, but still rather well-preserved ancient two-story structure --- Fagan's road ranch, the second scheduled stage stop on the Cheyenne-Black Hills road. During a March blizzard of 1876, some 250 travelers caught on the road found shelter there, filling the stables and outbuildings, as well as Michael Fagan's nine-room "hotel", to overflowing. This is the only early road ranch house we know of that is still standing, practically intact. It'd be a pity were it also to vanish from the stage of history.

From Fagan's, the old trail meanders back to the Cheyenne-Wheatland highway and crosses South Bear Creek some three miles further on. This was the site of Bard's Ranch, where Isaac Bard and his wife Rose started a roadside tavern in 1875, with some misgivings to judge by this entry in his diary: "I will now try keeping a public ranch for a year if the Good Lord is willing and the Indians will let me alone." Apparently, He was and they did. In 1877, Bard's became a regular stage station known as Little Bear.

Another eighteen miles or so further north, and a short distance east of the present village of Chugwater, is the site of John (Portugee) Phillips' popular road ranch of the 1870's, in a lush meadow beside the creek. A few piles of crumbled foundations, bits of rotted timber and iron, and a scattering of rusted square-headed nails are probably all you can find there. But its founder is fabled in song and story for perhaps the greatest, if not most famous, horseback ride in history. On December 21, 1866, impetuous Capt. William J. Fetterman and his command, eighty men in all, were waylaid by hostile Indians who enticed them over a ridge near Fort Phil Kearney (which Capt. Fetterman had been forbidden to cross), where they were slaughtered to a man. Several thousand tribesmen then laid siege to the small Post. Phillips, a civilian, volunteered to ride for help. He rode by night, hid by day, through blizzard and subzero weather, and reached Fort Laramie, 236 miles to the southeast, late Christmas eve. A hard story to believe --- but history says it is so.

Some fifteen miles further down the Chug and several miles east of the highway lies historic old Bordeaux, crossroads for travelers north, south, and east, and the home and headquarters of pioneer John Hunton. The buildings which were Bordeaux's trading post, erected in 1867, and Hunton's original road ranch, stage station, and post office, are gone. About all that remains is a small burial grounds near where they stood. We do not know the names of those who lie there. But the large two-story house John Hunton built for Blanche, his bride of the early 1880's, remains today a beautiful and well-kept ranch home.

A few miles beyond Bordeaux, the old road to Fort Laramie leaves Chugwater Creek and winds its way northeast. The first stop, after several miles of tortuous traveling, is Chug Springs (if you can find it). This was once the ranch of John Owens, [who was discussed in chapter 3].

Chug Springs is a sheltered nook on the prairie, a bit of an oasis still nurtured by a nest of moss-covered springs. The remains of a massive stone foundation more than a hundred feet long and some seventy-five feet wide is mute evidence that this now lonely and deserted spot once provided safe camp and shelter for thousands of gold-hungry travelers to the Black Hills and the hardy freighters of yesterday with their plodding teams of work cattle. It was also a favorite camping place for the troops who guarded their way. A few hundred yards beyond that stone foundation, the tiny valley is bordered by a rough and sudden cliff [where the half-breed Indian boy, Baptiste Ladeau, was killed, as described in chapter 1].

And it was at Chug Springs that your twentieth-century bull whackers almost had to make camp for the winter, or at least until some other unlikely traveler chanced along that ghostly way. The car keys became mysteriously lost. The area was searched and searched again --- no car keys. But Mr. Hildebrand did pick up one of the most beautiful bird arrowheads we have ever seen. It was perhaps three-quarters of an inch long and half as wide, a glistening pink, perfectly-shaped head of exquisite workmanship. Finally, when others had lost hope and were ready to quit, Mr. Bishop deployed his forces with engineering precision to cover every foot of the ground in a final and determined search. His persistence triumphed. The keys were found, coyly peeking out at us from their hiding place in that catch-all crack between the cushions of the car's front seat.

With our gas-powered stage coach ready to roll again, it became a question of finding our way back from Chug Springs to that oiled highway before snow and darkness trapped us in. We did. Shelter for the night was found in Wheatland, and there the expedition lost part of its equipment, namely, Mr. Bishop's suitcase, left nonchalantly behind next morning when we hit the road again. Mr. Bishop was not one to forget the hidden location of an historic site, and the course of a dim-covered wagon trail, once seen, was forever engraved on his memory --- but remembering such trivia as traveling bags and things like that was a different story. However, this mishap in no way slowed down the expedition's schedule.

From Chug Springs, the old road winds on another seven or eight miles to Eagle's Nest, but you have to travel much farther than that to reach it with modern transportation. This remarkable pioneer landmark lies not more than a mile off the now little-used country road south of the Laramie River between Wheatland and Fort Laramie. You will recognize it almost as far as you can see it. Those old timers had a flair for descriptive names. Two sheer cliffs rise out of the prairie. Between them is the Eagle's Nest with an entrance at either end. It was a desolate spot in the old days --- no wood, little grass, but there was a well of good water. Countless names on the walls of both cliffs show that thousands camped there through the years, or at least stopped to quench the thirst of man and beast. Many of those names were carved in the soft rock during 1877, heaviest year of the gold rush to the Black Hills. The earliest date noted in a brief examination was 1849. Since Eagle's Nest lies far off today's beaten tourist track and miles from a modern highway, this register from the past has fortunately escaped serious mutilation.

The Fort Laramie National Historic Site is some fifteen miles northeast of Eagle's Nest by the old trail, perhaps closer to twenty miles by today's road. A little more than half way there, you cross a draw which Mr. Hunton called Baptiste's Fork, now known as Six Mile Creek. The notorious Six Mile Ranch [spotlighted in chapter 3] once stood here --- the rendezvous of bad men, tough freighters, and soldiers on dubious pleasure bent, where old timers played it fast and rough, and life was, at times, a bit uncertain. But one would never guess at such goings-on from the neat ranch headquarters which marks the spot today.

A short distance west of Fort Laramie, at the edge of the old military reservation, are remains of the Three Mile Ranch, where soldiers and others who wished to join in the fun once cavorted in questionable forms of gaiety. The original site has been reduced to several mounds of rubble, with a few hand-riveted old barrel bands scattered around, and a remarkably preserved rock-walled well which could probably still be used with a little cleaning out. Albert Nietfeld, born on an adjoining place and the son of pioneer Henry Nietfeld, piloted us to this old well and also on the search for Eagle's Nest --- else we might still be looking for it.

On the north side of the Laramie, almost directly opposite the old well, is the later site of Three Mile. A long, narrow building with several closely-spaced, alternating doors and windows along its front, still stands in fairly good condition at this location. According to John Hunton, the structure was built in 1874 by Ecoffey and Cuny. So it must have been from these windows and doors that Mistress Calamity Jane and her professional sisters made their welcoming bows to the men of the west, [as noted in chapter 3], and no introductions necessary.

Before leaving the Fort Laramie area, our party stopped to chat with an old friend, Clement Ayers, who was busy forking hay to his cattle between Three Mile and the Old Fort. Mr. Ayers' stepfather, the late Alvah W. Ayers, was one of the big bull-train freighters in Wyoming Territory during the late 1870's and early 1880's. He kept careful records of distances between camps, of water, wood, and grass conditions along the trail, and other similar data essential to the operation of his business. Mr. Bishop used much of this information in preparing his maps and distance tables.

There was not much further search for old roads and places that afternoon. Something else developed which seemed even more important at the moment. A rumor sprang up that Mrs. Hildebrand had food and hospitality waiting for us in Douglas. This proved to be one of the most well-founded, robust, and savory rumors we have ever tasted. The food was followed by hours of solid talk in the warm glow of a fireplace, uninterrupted by games or gadgets. And nobody cared about January's blow and snow outside. An evening to remember.

From Douglas, a dim trail winds close by beautiful LaPrele Creek, past John Hunton's old Milk Ranch, and on to the site of Fort Fetterman, some eight or ten miles from town. Standing on the sage and brush-covered parade ground at that deserted place, it is hard to realize it once echoed to the military tread of perhaps the mightiest forces this nation ever mustered to send against the Sioux; that from Fort Fetterman streamed the long columns of General Crook's blue-uniformed troops with their thousands of horses, pack mules, and long supply wagon trains to finally subdue the tribesmen and make Black Hills' gold and the other wealth of Wyoming-Montana-Dakota mountains and plains safe for the white man, whether he deserved it or not. Only one sagging log structure and a few mounds of disintegrated rubble remain at the grave of this once-proud stronghold. An old

farmhouse, now likewise deserted, also stands there and em-
phasizes how far removed is Fort Fetterman's ancient glory.

A few miles further north on the old Bozeman Trail brings
you to the equally-desolate site of that once famous and infamous
Hog Ranch which flaunted its attractions at the edge of the
military reservation. No sign of sin or roistering gaiety there
today. Just a few littered dugouts where soldiers and freighters
once played and drank and fought to while away their leisure
time.

The Indians and road agents are long gone, but it is still a
rugged country from Fort Fetterman north along the ghostly
Bozeman Trail, past those vanished camps and stage stations at
Sage Creek, Brown Springs, Humpherville Creek (now known as
Stinking Water), Antelope Springs, and on to Powder River, with
Pumpkin Buttes, where outlaws once sought refuge when things
got too hot, looming up to the east. Perhaps the country seemed
a little extra rugged that day with the winter wind whistling,
hard snow pellets filling the air, and one hand kept busy scraping
holes through heavy frost on car windshield and windows to
peep through. But it is a great cattle and sheep range where the
term "wide open spaces" is no exaggeration.

On that drive of some 75 miles as the snake wiggles, we met
not more than half a dozen cars, saw perhaps as many ranch
headquarters looming dimly through the storm, passed one
empty and deserted roadside store, and a few distant bands of
hillside-bedded sheep --- that was all until we approached the
little town and ranching community of Sussex, near the Powder
River in southeastern Johnson county. Old Fort Reno, or at least
one of its sites, lies some eight or ten miles north of Sussex. This
frontier post seems to have had a habit of jumping around in the
area and of changing its name from time to time. Old records
show it as Fort Connor, Reno Fort, and later as "Fort Reno, Wyo,
on Powder River 3 miles north of old Fort Reno". There appears

to still be some question among authorities as to which is which. A granite marker erected by the Wyoming Historical Landmark Commission marks the site we visited --- otherwise, one could easily pass it by. Here there were traces of old structures and fortifications, but several inches of new snow prevented a close examination of the grounds.

On our way north from Fort Reno toward Crazy Woman Creek and old Fort McKinney (now Buffalo), the fun really began. A dim and by now snow-covered road wound and looped, with what seemed to be aimless abandon, from ridge to ridge under darkening skies. Along the way, we passed a lonely sheep wagon in which there was nobody home. It was the only sign of life observed for an hour or so. Differences of opinion on how we were doing developed. One held that we were traveling north most of the time and were therefore okay; another that we had somehow made a wrong turn and were headed south to the Lord knew where; while others stoutly maintained we were just chasing our own tail light round and round in a big circle. All agreed on one thing, that such a bunch of rugged trail followers as we could not possibly be lost. But as time went on, we became increasingly suspicious that someone had carelessly misplaced the town of Buffalo which we were so earnestly seeking.

Our arguments and apprehensions were settled at last by a dark-complected, ancient, and amiable gentleman with white mustachios who came chugging toward us out of the twilight with a jag of coal in his pickup --- headed cheerfully home to his band of sheep and that covered wagon we had passed way back yonder. He assured us if we would but follow his tracks, they would lead us where we wanted to go. And sure enough, before long we came to the oil highway and there, just over a hill, nestled Buffalo snugly as ever in her sheltered saucer among the hills. Lights from the old Occidental Hotel looked mighty warm and hospitable, and so they proved to be. Guests on the Clear

Creek side of the Occidental can cast a line from their bedroom windows and doubtless catch their own breakfast trout, but we understand they seldom do.

The proprietress of this historic hostelry was wife of the late Alfred E. Smith, whose father was "Captain" John R. Smith, hero of the Battle of Horse Shoe Creek. When pioneer John Smith was not too busy fighting Indians or shooting road agents, he gave John Hunton stiff competition in the business of selling beef and hay to Uncle Sam's northern frontier posts.

Mrs. Smith and her son graciously invited our party to visit them in their hotel apartment that evening, and some great old tales were retold. She came to Buffalo as Margaret Lothian and recalled how a pioneer rancher of that day, Jack Moore, helped kindle the fires of romance between school teacher Margaret and her Alfred-to-be. As we recall the story, rancher Moore, who was the father of novelist Olga Moore Arnold, made a small bet with young rancher Alfred Smith that he could not date the school marm and bring her out to Thanksgiving dinner. Smith won the bet, the dinner, and a bride to boot. And that was probably one bet Jack Moore did not mind losing, for he is remembered as a peppery gentleman in politics, but kindly and perhaps a bit sentimental in person, especially where young school teachers were concerned.

Fort McKinney, close by Buffalo, is now the Wyoming Soldiers and Sailors Home --- a peaceful spot, with fat Black Angus cattle pasturing the surrounding bottoms and meadow land, and a far cry from the savage war-whoops which gave it birth.

From Fort McKinney, the old trail winds north through beautiful, well-watered valleys shadowed by the snow-capped Big Horns, never straying far from U. S. Highway 87. Historic sites along the way are mostly well-marked, if not always well-kept. They include: Fort Phil Kearney, a short distance from today's town of Story; nearby Massacre Hill, where rash Capt. Fetterman and his command met death; the approximate site of that famous Wagon Box fight where the Indians, in their turn, took a bad beating; Fort McKenzie, now the Veterans Administration Hospital on the outskirts of Sheridan; and so on to the Custer Battle Field national monument and cemetery in southern Montana, which alone is worth the trip if one has never seen it.

It now became necessary to hurry back from the fields of yesterday to the more pressing, if not more interesting, business of today. From Buffalo through Midwest to Casper, the old, old trails show frequently on both sides of the new super-duper highway, provided you know when and where to look for them. And those rolling plains between Midwest and Casper were familiar ground to Engineer Bishop, who surveyed over them many years ago in the early oil discovery days, when it was necessary to travel by wagon, buggy, and horseback. He recalled that many of the original section corners of that day were marked by piles of buffalo skulls. They were plentiful then, while suitable rocks were often few and far between.

Such a trip is good medicine, especially if one is inclined to take today's current and personal affairs more seriously than they deserve. Makes you realize they, too --- for all their present importance, pain, and pleasure --- will likewise soon pass and fade down the long corridor of time as have the red warchiefs, the frontiersmen, and the blue-coated cavalry who were here and occupied this stage before us.

L . G . (Pat) Flannery
- Historian, Statesman, Writer Extraordinaire -

L. G. (Pat) Flannery was born on March 3, 1894, in St. Louis, Missouri. He attended school in St. Louis and Chicago prior to moving to Denver, Colorado with his parents in 1912. He attended high school in Denver and later enrolled in the old Colorado State College of Agriculture at Fort Collins, Colorado. (There he courted Laura Alice Moomaw, married her, and in 1916, Alice gave birth to their daughter and only child, Billie.)

In 1921, Mr. Flannery moved, with his wife and daughter, to Fort Laramie, Wyoming, where he engaged in ranching. In 1923, he founded a weekly newspaper, the *Fort Laramie Scout*, which he later combined with the *Goshen County News* in Torrington, Wyoming. Its files contain some of the choicest editorial writing ever seen in print.

In the following years, Mr. Flannery became a leader in political circles in Wyoming, serving as state chairman of his party, during which time the party won its greatest election victories in the state. He was a member of the state legislature from Goshen County and served as secretary of the State Board of Charities and Reform, and at one time was director of the State Department of Commerce and Industry. Pat spent a year in Washington, D. C. in the Information Service under Harry Hopkins prior to his appointment as State Administrator of the Works Progress Administration for Wyoming. He resigned this high-salaried government post to enlist as a $21-a-month private in World War II. (Pat was also a veteran of World War I.)

Following his discharge from the army, Flannery became supervisor of the U. S. Agriculture Census for Wyoming and Colorado. In 1947, he was appointed the Administrative Assistant to Wyoming's Senator O'Mahoney in Washington, D. C. He served this post for six years and then retired from politics in 1953.

Mr. Flannery had long owned the homestead site of his old friend, John Hunton, at Fort Laramie. It was here that he retired and spent the last several years of his interesting life organizing and editing the John Hunton diaries for publication, with a valuable four-volume set completed and published before his death on February 4, 1964. (His wife, Alice, then pursued the publication of two more volumes based on manuscripts Pat had in his files.)

Mr. Flannery will long be remembered for his political achievements, and even more widely known for his writing and knowledge of early Wyoming history.

www.ingramcontent.com/pod-product-compliance
Lightning Source LLC
Chambersburg PA
CBHW070920270326
41927CB00011B/2662